BAD TRIP

An inside view of the ride share industry

by

Chris Poindexter

Copyright © 2017 Chris Poindexter

All rights reserved.
Cover art by Aaron Rosen www.pixel-mesh.com

ISBN:
ISBN-13:

DEDICATION

To Shangsta, SteveK2016 and so many other drivers who are everyday heroes and deserve better than they're getting today.

.Table of Contents

Introduction..1
Ride Share – The Early Years......................8
Qualities of a Good Driver........................16
The Car..24
Accessories – Outfitting Your Car................37
Insurance...45
The Ratings Game..................................50
Factors Impacting Income.........................54
The Mode Ride and Theoretical Maximum.......64
The Real Numbers...................................75
Figuring In Expenses...............................84
The Cloud of Disinformation.....................89
Pool and Line – Welcome To Hell.................98
Optimization Strategies............................103
Muddying The Waters 126
Risk Factors...131
Annoying Passenger Tricks.........................141
The Fatal Flaw...150
Questions & Answers 162
About The Author....................................171

INTRODUCTION

Ride sharing is one of the more disruptive technologies of the modern era of transportation. The concept is simple, convenient and, at least in the beginning, egalitarian. You have a car and that car has more seats than you use. Ride sharing allows you to monetize those empty seats by offering rides to people who need to get from Point A to Point B. At that basic level is where facts end and disinformation begins. Currently the ride sharing industry is steeped in misinformation and people trying to make a decision about whether to participate are doing so most often on a flawed and incomplete base of knowledge. That brings us to rule number one when considering participating in the industry:

Ambiguity is not your friend

Some of the misinformation floating around out there is deliberate; some of it is being shared by the well-meaning but misinformed. Bad Trip – An inside view of the ride share industry is an effort to cut through the cloud of misinformation and give people contemplating ride sharing as a job or a sideline a better foundation for making a decision. During my own investigation into ride sharing, I ran into the propaganda of the cheerleaders, some of which I believe is planted by the companies themselves or their online surrogates. I also found a lot of disillusioned drivers.

To avoid trademark issues or typing the same names over and over I'm not going to mention the actual names of any ride share companies. Instead I will refer to two possibly fictional but very realistic companies represented by the letters U and L. If those were real companies, I'm certain you could probably figure out which is which.

The concept of this book is to share the total reality of my experience in the ride share industry. The view will include the driving, the passengers, insurance, income and expenses. I'll document both my approach and decision process, so you can avoid my mistakes. We'll cover the qualities that make a good driver and you can decide for yourself how much of that description fits you. I'll also go over the indirect income aspects, like tipping and ratings, so you can decide whether it's worth your time and the associated risks, which are not insignificant.

Most people come here wanting nothing more than to find out how much money they can make. If that's you I encourage you to read the whole book anyway, so you have a more complete idea of what you're getting into driving ride share. In my experience money was, ultimately, not the biggest consideration. Income is the question everyone wants to answer but that's one layer of many when it comes to driving. If I'm doing my job here many will reach a conclusion of whether ride share driving is right for them based on issues other than money.

To get good data about how much money you can actually make driving for either of the two major ride share companies, I tried as much as possible to run my ride sharing efforts like a real business. I bought a car specifically for ride sharing and didn't use it for it for any personal business or trips. In addition I used a separate bank account to track income and expenses and tracked mileage using a phone app tied to a bookkeeping program. I tracked my earnings per hour both in terms of passenger clock hours and real time. I also tracked my actual earnings per hour, whether I'm online with the ride share app or not. Neither U nor L want to recognize actual earnings per hour, even though their human drivers have to take a bio break once in a while, pump gas and eat. In the ride share business all those activities take away from your potential earnings.

Finally, I'll delve into the strategies for maximizing your income as a driver, which are not all intuitive. Some of those suggestions will put you at odds with the company philosophy on some elements of conducting yourself as a driver. What I've noticed is that, eventually, the company will adapt to driver strategies to thwart those policies. The driver application, payment calculations and profit strategies are changing constantly. What works today might not work next month and you need to be prepared to adapt. In addition, there is a strong suspicion of undocumented "features" in the software application itself which may be collecting data far beyond a driver's behavior behind the wheel. It recently came to light that one company was tracking law enforcement and sending them phony information. Any company that would do that to law enforcement certainly has no qualms about deceiving you.

Lately the news has been full of stories about drivers sleeping in parking lots in order to make a living. I am here to testify that those stories are accurate and, as we go through the book, you'll learn why some drivers have been moved to those extremes. But first this warning:

Before I get to the answer you probably came here to get, let me remind you of a scene from the Hitchhiker's Guide to the Galaxy. A group of scientists build a giant computer, called Deep Thought, so they could ask it to compute the answer to life, the universe and everything. Deep Thought's first answer to that question:

Tricky

That answer is bizarrely appropriate to this discussion and the reason you'll find numbers all over the map when researching ride share earnings. Deep Thought's second answer to the question, which took millions of years to figure out, was even more annoying. When asked if the machine finally had the answer, Deep Thought said:

You're really not going to like it

The scientists, who had waited generations for the answer, finally discovered Deep Thought's answer which, if you've read the book, you already know is 42. As the machine predicted, the scientists didn't like it. I dragged you through that story to make a point which is that I will give you the answer but it's tricky, it's going to take a long time to explain (it will seem like 7.5 million years) and you're not going to like it. The answer also involves math, which seems to intimidate many. There's no avoiding that, unfortunately, so dust off that old calculator and follow along.

So, with that, here's the short answer you've come here to find. After hundreds of hours driving, painfully and methodically entering every trip into a spreadsheet, thousands of miles behind the wheel and tracking every penny of expense, the answer to how much money you can make:

It depends

Disappointed? Don't be. It just means that the complete answer is more complicated than you thought and there are a lot of variables that influence how much you can make. We'll spend the rest of the book explaining that answer, including some real life numbers.

One thing I should point out. If this is the print version you might have noticed a QR code that looked like this:

That's because the text is dotted with references. In the ebook version you can create URLs and click to follow the link right in the copy. In print books your readers have to laboriously type them out by hand. For that reason I converted the URLs to QR codes in the print version so all you have to do is scan them with a reader to call up the reference on your phone or tablet. Over time web links can go stale or break. If you find a broken link, copy error or math mistake, please use the author contact information in the About The Author section at the end of the book to let me know.

Another thing about the copy is it may seem duplicative in spots. That's often due to the fact that a topic fits into the discussion in more than one category. Instead of eliminating any overlap or duplication, I decided to just leaving it in the context of that chapter. For example, surge fares appear in Factors Impacting Income, The Real Numbers and Optimization Strategies. The topic is relevant to each of them but in a slightly different way.

There's also some disagreement in the literary world whether the term is ride share or rideshare. Instead of picking a side in the debate, I just use ride share and ride sharing in the book copy but you'll notice I use both terms in the jacket and book description. That's because people search for the term both ways. Also the AP bans the term ride-sharing altogether and now uses the term ride-hailing instead but it's not in common use, but that won't stop me from using it in my search keywords.

And with that, we're ready to start our journey. Fasten your seatbelt and there's no eating, drinking or smoking in the vehicle...wait, that's for the car. You can eat, drink or smoke as much as you like reading the book...unless you're in the back of a U or L car while reading this.

RIDE SHARING – THE EARLY YEARS

In the beginning were taxi cabs. Sure, we could go back further to stagecoaches but that was more like modern buses than ride sharing. Taxis were the Mark I ride sharing service and quickly grew to be an integral transportation service in metropolitan areas. Over time the taxi industry became entrenched and big players sought standards and licensing that kept smaller competitors out of the market. Taxis thrived specifically because they were able to regulate competition and prices went up and up.

The first time I remember hearing about ride sharing was the 1960s and 1970s. Perhaps I'm dating myself but back then ride sharing was basically holding up a sign with your destination next to the road and hoping some kind soul would take pity on you and give you a lift in that general direction. There was no communication with the driver prior to them stopping, rarely was money involved and there were no apps to score either passenger or driver. There was also no protection for either the driver or passenger and, sometimes, the trip went poorly for one or the other.

In New York in 1980, during a transit strike, people started hauling their neighbors around town in vans and delivery trucks for a couple bucks called Dollar Vans. The transit strike went on for just short of two weeks but the underground travel system, called Shadow Transit, continued on in neighborhoods that were not well-served by public transportation. The vans managed to stay in business and even became regulated entities in some places but mainly they existed in spite of sometimes heavy-handed police and regulatory efforts to stop them. Modern ride sharing, in many ways, owes its existence to the old Dollar Vans.

Today ride sharing is a fusion of several technologies: GPS, mobile data, credit card payments and the increasing miniaturization of computer technology. Originally ride share companies were merely matchmakers, pairing up people with cars with other people who needed rides in exchange for keeping a small part of the transaction cost. It was easy, it was seamless and it was cool watching the little car icon getting closer on the map on your phone. During my first ride on U, I remember feeling like I'd just discovered fire. It was brilliant.

That simple concept was a direct challenge to taxi operators, who believe ride sharing is cheating. They believe it skirts the rules of running a transportation business. It wasn't that long ago that taxi medallions, what you once needed to operate a cab, cost thousands of dollars and came with a great deal of oversight by state, county and local government.

Modern ride sharing technology exposed taxi

cabs to be an archaic system weighed down by overhead that provided little real value. The safety of modern vehicles has improved to the point that a simple safety inspection by a qualified mechanic can verify that the car you're riding in is safe transportation.

Yet safety was the banner local governments hoisted when first fighting back against the nascent ride share industry. City and county officials downloaded the ride share apps and used them to lure drivers to fines, vehicle impoundment and, sometimes, arrest. All of that enforcement effort was done in the name of safety, but it wasn't really about safety, it was about turf and kickbacks and control. With taxi services costing nearly $3.00 a mile and not serving many areas, what local officials learned quickly was that people liked ride sharing better than they liked elected officials. Enforcement was difficult and, considering the stealthy nature of ride sharing, the industry was challenging to regulate. Courts didn't like officials using the app to trap people and prosecuting individual drivers was like trying to stop the wind. In the early days ride share drivers made a lot of money and the lure kept new drivers lining up to take the place of those whose cars had been impounded.

To meet the local threat, companies like U and L had to step out of the middleman role and take point in the negotiations with local regulators. At least in South Florida most of those negotiations were taking place in early 2014. By that time the companies had grown, a lot, and local regulators found themselves overmatched by sheer, raw corporate power. The moment was significant because it marks the time U transformed from a middleman to a brand; even their name became a verb.

Eventually, and one at a time, cities, counties and municipalities knuckled under to the inevitable and cut individual deals with U, which usually included vehicle safety inspections and, due to a few isolated incidents with problem drivers, background checks for drivers became mandatory. Those background checks, though not perfect, could screen out people with poor driving records and felony convictions.

It was at this pivotal point that U began to transform and changed from a middleman to a brand and the brand into a transportation empire. What we're seeing today, in my opinion, is the decline and eventual collapse of that empire. That sad transformation has happened before in technology. AOL, which brought thousands of people online, is a service only old people remember today. Dell is another example. Dell owned the personal computer market in 2004 but lost that dominant position when they stopped doing the things that got them to the top.

Like AOL and Dell, U has stopped doing the things that made it great and has adopted a pattern of behavior that, I believe, will lead to its undoing. I discovered that fatal flaw, which I'll document in later chapters, the very first week I started driving for them. The inevitability of that eventual decline is kind of a bummer because I really like the ride share concept and what will take its place when it eventually passes into tech history will be something else.

For all its apparent faults, the giant of the ride share industry still gets credit as the pioneer of a new industry and a bold forward step in combining transportation and technology. But, as one of my business mentors used to remind me, pioneers are the people lying out in the prairie full of arrows and U has definitely had to weather its share of setbacks. The company's survival is by no means certain and, I believe, they won't make it.

When we discuss the ride share industry today, it's really a tale of two distinct eras: The era before 2014 and the time frame after 2014. It wasn't a sharp change, like a curtain coming down, but more of a transition zone that started in 2014 and flowed through 2015. The industry changes since then have been continuous, though less dramatic. In that time frame we watched ride sharing undergo explosive growth but not all the changes were for the better.

In the early days, ride sharing was a community that grew out of the sharing economy. Service was by mutual agreement between the passenger and the driver. Passengers who were rude or uncaring didn't last in the community atmosphere. The voluntary nature of the relationship and the community aura kept drivers invested in the success of the service and passengers on their best behavior. In the early days ride sharing worked precisely because it wasn't a mass market product and both riders and drivers were occasionally dropped from participation because they didn't fit in.

The Great Transition in ride sharing started in 2014 when the company was forced to step into the role of dealing with regulators as the industry continued to grow at a startling pace. That meant more overhead at the corporate level and the company paid for that expansion by cutting driver pay by slashing rates. That was a big mistake and the company decided to repeat that mistake again in 2015, along with raising the percentage the company held back as its share. To add insult to injury, the company insisted in public statements that cutting rates was actually helping drivers make more money. That statement is proof of the old business logic that says if you're going to lie, go big.

That's also about the time both companies started tinkering with self-driving cars and promoting services like Line and Pool, where riders going the same direction could share a car. Pool and Line are universally hated by drivers and, surprisingly, by many passengers who sometimes accidentally pick Pool because the rider app defaults to that choice in some markets. I had a French-Canadian couple in the car one day who were using their best English to try and describe a horror trip they had on Pool. More on that in the chapter entitled Pool and Line - Welcome To Hell. All of those changes drastically changed the ride share landscape as you'll see when we get to later chapters.

My journey to understand ride sharing began with an article I did for a news site. I wanted to include ride sharing in a list of ways people could work to earn extra money. What I discovered researching that article was that the answers to how much you could make driving were all over the road (come on, you know that pun was too good to pass up). I could not find a consistent answer to what should have been a relatively simple question.

The question nagged at me for weeks afterwards and I kept doing research on the side, trying to understand the business. Clear answers eluded me and what I discovered was a sheer wall of disinformation that was difficult to penetrate. As I collected research, I decided to compile that information, perhaps for an in-depth article at a later date. Like an old chuck steak, the more I chewed on the story, the bigger it got. I spent a lot of time in driver forums where I expected to find answers. Instead what I found was more disinformation and confusion.

The questions remained unanswered and, eventually, I decided the only way I was going to get the real answers I was seeking was to join the community of drivers and collect real life data. That effort was more time-consuming and way more expensive than I anticipated. Even after I started driving I discovered the need to keep fairly detailed records to understand my earnings.

What I learned was that the answers were hard to find because they are complicated. In this book I've made an effort to simplify the calculations. Anyone with a calculator and some basic background information can make a fairly accurate guess about how much they can make driving for either of the major ride share companies. As part of evaluating whether that income is worth your time, I'll also cover the risks and downsides, which are not insignificant. The basic premise of being in business for yourself is Risk vs Reward. Those who take the risks get the rewards. That basic rule may not apply the same way in the ride share industry.

The answers were out there but I had to drive for nearly a month before finally being able to separate the good information from the disinformation. I urge you not to skip the background material and go straight to the numbers because you also need to understand the context of the income numbers. I will give you the tools to figure out the answers you need but that doesn't mean it's easy.

QUALITIES OF A GOOD DRIVER

One of my first jobs as an adult in South Florida was driving a delivery van for a local auto supply company. That was when South Florida was still growing and was, in many ways, a calmer and more sedate place. All the same I learned to navigate Florida streets, Florida traffic and, most importantly, Florida drivers at an early age. I enjoy driving, I'm good at it and routinely get compliments from passengers about how much they appreciate the smooth ride.

I wanted to put this section near the front because it's possible you may see that you're not the right kind of person for the job and you can skip the rest of the book. Believe me when I say that this job is not for everyone. If you're not suited for the work, don't do it. Here are the qualities that make really great drivers.

Predictability

The best drivers understand that traffic has a flow and how to go with it. The most valuable quality a driver can have behind the wheel is predictability. Drivers who get in trouble, both with the law and other drivers, are those behaving aggressively and unpredictably.

Unpredictability doesn't necessarily extend from aggression. The most unpredictable drivers here in Florida are tourists. They're trying to navigate unfamiliar territory and the human brain has limits on how much information it can process at any one time. Take a few disoriented tourists, add in a couple aggressive dirtbags and sprinkle with the well-meaning but inept and you have a formula for some of the worst traffic and highest insurance rates anywhere in the country. If you can drive here, you can drive anywhere. The same is true with cities like Boston, Atlanta, New York, Chicago and L.A. If you can survive in any of those swirling cauldrons of steel, then you'll probably be fine as a ride share driver.

Keep in mind that you make the most money when there are more cars on the road, which means taking on traffic and difficult driving situations is the job.

Patience

The worst quality you can have as a driver is impatience. Impatience can lead to speeding, tailgating and aggressive behaviors behind the wheel. If you drive aggressively with passengers in the car, you will see your driver rating decline very quickly. Passengers don't like aggressive drivers and it reflects poorly on the industry. In my experience interviewing other people in the ride share industry, those who are a little older make the best drivers. You can't let a couple bucks motivate your driving, especially when it comes to speeding.

Let's take an example of a 60 mile trip, which is roughly the distance from here to Miami

International Airport. The speed limit for most of that trip is 65 mph, both on I-95 and Florida's Turnpike. The math looks like this:

Distance = Speed * Time

We want to know how many minutes a trip would take driving the speed limit versus driving at 75 or 80 mph. To make that comparison we need to convert all our time units to minutes. So...

65 mph is 1.08 miles per minute

75 mph is 1.25 miles per minute

80 mph is 1.333 miles per minute.

You can already see there's not a huge difference in those numbers. Now that we have equalized the time values we can make some comparisons.

60 miles = 1.08 miles per minute * Time

Solving for Time we get.

60/1.08 = 55.5 minutes

That was nearly perfectly the time on my last airport run to Miami. It took me a bit longer to get there because of traffic but it was right in that range. Now we can see how much difference adding 10 mph to your speed makes.

75 mph = 1.25 miles per minute

60/1.25 = 48 minutes

And for 80 mph.

60/1.33 = 45 minutes

There you have it. Going 15 mph over the speed limit, risking a ticket and getting in an accident, only buys you 10 extra minutes. Going ten over the speed limit only buys you seven minutes. When you start looking at the actual numbers it becomes clear that speeding is simply not worth the associated risks. The icing on the cake is that, in most states, if you're speeding you forfeit any right of way, meaning that you'll greatly increase the likelihood that you'll be found at fault for any accident. These days the police can pull the car's speed, engine performance and driver reaction time from your vehicle's computer, so they don't even have to be there to know how fast you were going.

Only occasionally will a customer encourage me to break the speed limit and, when they do, I review the math of speeding for them. Once they realize the difference is only three or four minutes, they usually drop it. If they keep on I give them the option of canceling the trip and hailing another driver. That process would certainly take longer than any time saved convincing the next driver to speed.

Remain Calm

Florida drivers are experts at raising your blood pressure. If you start yelling and sending hand signals when you have passengers in the car it will terrify your passengers and jeopardize their safety. Sometimes it's my passengers cursing and gesturing at other cars and I have to remind them that I still have to drive next to these people after they go home.

When it's just you, if you want to go off on another driver that's your business. When you have passengers in the car, then you have a duty of care to them and you need to remain calm. Definitely don't do anything that could be seen as escalating a conflict. The situation won't be as clear when you're trying to explain it to the police.

Be Reasonable

Another good quality of a driver is being reasonable. Reasonable means you're flexible without being a pushover. Passengers will take advantage of drivers if they can but most will relent in the face of reasonableness. One of the most frequent points of potential conflict is passengers wanting to bring food and drinks in the car. Some drivers will cancel passengers with any type of food or beverage container. My rules are drinks must have a lid and stay in the drink holder and food has to stay in the bag. I'll let them bring food in a bag but there's no eating in my car. To me that seems reasonable. On one occasion a passenger had a pink drink that would look really bad on my car seats. I told her I'd wait, off the clock, until she finished it and, if it spilled in the car, there would be a $25 cleaning fee.

More often passengers will try to bring alcohol into the car. I learned my first day on the job to keep the doors locked until we reach an understanding on the booze or beer issue. Unfortunately, there's no room to budge on this one here in Florida. There are no open containers of alcohol allowed in my car ever. Again, being a little reasonable can help diffuse an uncomfortable situation. I'll offer to wait while they finish their beer and give them the option of canceling the ride and calling another car. The vast majority of the time they'll take a couple last gulps and toss the rest rather than stand around. If they get pissy or belligerent with me then I'll cancel the ride and drive away. Fortunately, I'm a large man and that alone heads off a lot of potential conflict.

Just like with kids, giving passengers choices smooths over a lot of potential conflicts. It's a better idea to let them choose between waiting and bringing their beer rather than just saying no.

Clarity

Many ride share drivers do not speak English as a native language and conflicts can arise due to miscommunication with passengers. I've found that being clear and consistent with passengers is the best way to keep misunderstandings at a minimum. If you need to clarify something with passengers, try to do it before you start the drive. Don't talk to the windshield. Turn around, make eye contact and calmly explain what you need to tell them. Do not try to stop and explain something to a passenger after you start the trip. If I have to stop the car then it should only be something bad enough to kick them out.

When I'm driving in Miami that turns the communication dynamic upside down. The majority of people in the Miami/Dade area speak Spanish and many don't speak English at all. If you live an area like that then learn a few simple phrases and directions. It doesn't sound like much but it provides my Spanish speaking customers with a bit of confidence knowing they can at least communicate where to turn and where to stop.

You Have To Like People

One of my passengers was a graphic artist meeting her boyfriend to watch the boat parade in Jupiter, Florida. My passenger was a graphic artist instead of a ride share driver because she's not a people person. People who thrive in lone wolf professions should consider carefully whether driving for a ride share company is a good idea. I took on this job primarily for the book but also because writing is a very isolating occupation. Driving forces me to mix it up and interact with other people in meatspace. I get along with the vast majority of my customers because I like people and find them interesting.

I discovered early on that I was actually out of practice communicating with other human beings face to face. It took me the better part of a week before I got that groove back and began to get more comfortable interacting with my passengers. Many don't want conversation. They've been interacting with people at work all day and all they want to do is veg out on their phone with headphones. Those people, I'll engage enough to acknowledge them, but after that I'll turn the radio down and give them their alone time. Most of the time, after about ten minutes of solitude, they'll start talking to me. All they needed was a few minutes to relax and regroup and then their social instincts kick in again. If you're a good observer, over time you'll get intuitive interacting with people.

If you don't like people, don't drive a ride share car. I can't make it any clearer than that simple statement.

You Have To Be Able To Say No...And Mean It

Some people are so afraid of rejection or a bad rating that they let customers walk all over them, which is both dangerous and unhealthy. Part of being a good driver is knowing where to draw the line and say no. It's vital in those situations that you don't make threats that you're not prepared to carry out.

The hair trigger of driver ratings can make you crazy but a bad driver rating is better than an expensive judgement so always maintain perspective. U will let you be deactivated for a low driver rating, even if those low ratings stem from stopping customers from doing something dangerous or illegal. One driver in New York City let a couple have sex in his SUV during a ride home because that was better than risking a low driver rating. His major complaint about that incident was that the woman left her chewing gum on the backseat.

Losing your ride share gig is better than years of dragging around a citation and higher insurance rates. Customers will let you get in trouble and they might feel bad but that won't translate into any relief for you. Rule number one in ride share driving and the most important piece of advice you'll ever get:

Protect yourself

The risks associated with ride share driving are not insignificant and the margins are thin. There's no margin in risking a ticket, lawsuit or getting in an accident. Protecting yourself from potential liability is far more important than keeping a crappy job. You can always find another job but a judgement can haunt you for life and, perhaps ironically, make it difficult getting future employment.

If you think you have those personality qualities and can act with determination to minimize risk, then let's move on to the nuts and bolts of finding the right car and getting your kit together.

THE CAR

The car you drive in your ride share adventure will be one of the most important decisions you make. I spent weeks shopping for my car and made numerous test drives. Later in this chapter I'll share all the cars I evaluated and whether they made the cut. There are four basic factors you'll balance out when choosing your car:

Vehicle Cost

Vehicle Operating Cost

Interior Space

Reliability

This first and most important decision you'll make will also move ride sharing from the theoretical to the reality of the business. Thus far we've been treating ride sharing like a single, monolithic service. In fact, there are several service levels inside U's operating framework and now we have to take a look at those service levels. Keep in mind these names change nearly constantly and not all levels of service are available in all areas. If that isn't confusing enough, sometimes the same service levels have different names.

U-X

This is U's basic ride sharing service and the cheapest service U offers. Most 4 door late model cars that are in good mechanical shape and don't have any obvious external damage will qualify. Your car must be capable of carrying four passengers besides the driver. The service is called U-Pop in Europe and will be cars like the Toyota Prius, Honda Fit and other 4 door sedans and hatchbacks. Since U-X is the lowest cost service, the goal here is to minimize your upfront costs and operating expenses.

I know several drivers taking U-X rides in SUVs and pickup trucks. To me that seems absolutely crazy. Maybe they can get by doing that when gas is $2.19 a gallon, the price here in South Florida at this writing, but those gas prices are not going to last. Bad gas mileage will absolutely kill your profit margin.

U-XL

U's XL service requires you can carry up to 6 passengers besides the driver. These would be large SUVs with third row seating and minivans. XL service costs more than X. Passengers are more than happy to let you break the law. There have been many times passengers wanted to try and squeeze 5 people into my Prius, including one guy who wanted to let his minor daughter sit on his lap. I said no way on that and asked him to cancel the ride and call for an XL. He may have but it's also just as likely he called another U-X and tried to con the driver into risking a ticket.

Based on my interviews of other drivers, XL

drivers make more than X drivers on a consistent basis. The higher income is balanced out, to a certain extent, by higher expenses. Also keep in mind the profit margin for XL will decline with rising gas prices.

U-LUX

Lux is U's luxury service and would include high end cars, like Mercedes, BMW and Audi that are no later than 2010 models with leather seats and professional drivers. This class includes unique cars like the Tesla Model S. This is a premium service that comes at a premium cost. It's been difficult to get good data on how much Lux drivers can make because there are fewer of them. The competition with limo services is more keen but, until limo services get away from those awful online service aggregators who add their own fees to the cost of a limo, U-LUX is going to eat their lunch. Generally, with premium services, you make more while working less often.

U-LUX SUV

This would be 2010 and later luxury SUVs and limos capable of carrying at least 6 passengers besides the driver. Vehicles like the Cadillac Escalade are a popular choice for LUX SUV service. I'll tell you right up front that I don't have good earnings data on LUX because most of the drivers also work for other commercial limo or transportation services.

Your Car Strategy

If you already have a qualifying car, you can skip this section. Otherwise, prepare for a lot of decisions that will ultimately have a large bearing on your likelihood of success.

Your car strategy is basically to get the most

functional vehicle, with the most interior space, for the least amount of money. If you're running your ride share venture like a business, then you need to consider depreciation and I need to define that term before we go any further because it gets tossed around a lot in driver forums and it's clear that many don't understand the concept. Most are using the term as it applies to the declining value of their car due to age and mileage, but that's not how the term applies in business.

In business, you need to operate your car as income producing machinery. Here's a brief overview of the IRS guidelines on depreciation and, from that document comes the definition of depreciation as I'm using it here:

Depreciation begins when a taxpayer places property in service for use in a trade or business or for the production of income. The property ceases to be depreciable when the taxpayer has fully recovered the property's cost or other basis or when the taxpayer retires it from service, whichever happens first.

The idea behind a depreciable asset is that a certain portion of the item's value can be used to offset the amount of taxes you have to pay on business income. The reason this is important is because leasing can throw off your tax calculation. In that case you have to understand the difference between different types of leases and that's way too far down in the tax weeds for this book.

If you're running a ride share car like a business, then do yourself a favor and get a good tax person and pay for a consult before you make a decision on how to acquire your vehicle. That will be money well spent. I totally get that some of these tax discussions are boring enough to make your eyes bleed but it's important to your bottom line. Skip those if you want, but you may regret doing so at the end of the year.

Cost

I went with a more expensive car than I needed because, once I get done with the book, it's not at all clear if I'm going to keep driving. For me, I'll either sell it to another aspiring ride share driver or keep it to commute to my next writing assignment. I'll make that decision when the time comes.

The most effective car strategy for U-X involves finding the cheapest car under 10 years old that can pass inspection and, literally, driving it into the ground. There are many hardcore U drivers putting a $10,000 limit on what they'll spend on a car. Having a fender bender in the vehicle history or already having a lot of miles on it doesn't matter to the really pro drivers. If you cruise the driver forums you can even find people looking at cars in the $2,000 to $3,000 dollar range.

Any car you pick should look nice on the outside. Don't worry about minor imperfections in the seats or interior, those can't be seen from the outside and you're going to invest in a quality set of seat covers anyway. Do be a little cautious if the vehicle has been in a previous accident. A minor fender bender is generally not a problem but a major accident with significant damage may disqualify your car.

I paid nearly $20,000 for my U-X car (including tax, title and license) which would be crazy were I not contemplating using it after I'm done driving. This is a business and you have to make a business decision when choosing a ride share car if that's the only way you're using it.

Do keep your options for a seven passenger vehicle open and explore that angle carefully. XL drivers tend to make more and drive longer. Your expenses will be higher but, if you have somewhere convenient where you can wait without driving around, you'll make more when you do work. I went with the X service level because of the car, no other reason.

Vehicle Age

Your aunt's old Toyota Camry may have less than 30,000 original miles but that doesn't mean it's a good choice for a ride share car. Most luxury models have to be 2010 or newer and you may not be able to get older cars on the system. Some cities and counties where ride share companies operate put limits on the vehicle's age. Many 2006 model year cars will be falling off the system by the time this book is out. Anything older than 10 years is probably going to be a no go.

A Dual Use Vehicle

The strategy changes somewhat if you plan on using your car for ride sharing part-time and getting back and forth to your day job. Then lease or car payments are already figured into your budget and ride sharing is merely extra income. The vehicle requirements remain the same but you may opt for a newer model year, lower miles and a higher price tag.

It also changes the math on the deduction of business mileage and expenses. If the car is doing double duty for both business and personal use, then you have to keep good mileage records to demonstrate to the IRS when the car is being used for commercial purposes and when you're on your own time.

A dual use vehicle is likely going to be newer with fewer miles than a car you purchase strictly for ride sharing.

Brands and Models I Considered

I looked at virtually every small, 4 door car on the used car market. Several models floated to the top of my list:

Toyota Prius Hybrid

The Prius is sort of the flagship of ride sharing services. They are moderately priced, extremely thrifty on gas, reliable and roomy. What I didn't realize was the Prius comes in several models, all priced differently. I ruled out the Prius C due to the fact that the roof slopes downward in the back and that cramps the headroom in the rear seats. The Prius C just felt cramped compared to other models.

When I tested the backseat in cars, myself and another 6'3, 280 pound man parked ourselves in the back and measured the distance between us, checked the headroom and knee room available. Then I'd have my wife sit between us with the doors closed. Believe me when I say that we got some extremely strange looks.

I'm glad I made that effort because it really did help eliminate some cars that had uncomfortable back seats. Strangely, that weeding out process included some models of the Prius, as noted up above.

Honda Accord Sedan

It's only by superhuman will that I don't type "Acorn" for that car name because that's what I call them. The Acorn....sorry, Accord...was a late addition to the car list and kind of an accident.

One of the places we shopped had one in the showroom and I was checking it out while we waiting for our salesperson.

I was surprised at how plush and comfortable it was. Even with the driver's seat back to where I was comfortable there was plenty of room in the backseat. That extra legroom in the back was a side effect of bucket rear seats. While really plush and comfortable that rear seat design made the back center seat a bit uncomfortable. It was clear that Honda didn't expect that rear middle seat to actually be used because engineers put a fold down drink holder there.

As comfortable as it was, and $2,000 cheaper than other cars we were looking at, the Acorn (just go with it) fell out due to gas mileage and the fact the interior had this weird herringbone pattern to it. It also lacked a backup camera and, trust me when I say, you'll want that backup camera. All the same, if you already have an Accord, go with it.

The backseat design was more important than I anticipated. You'll be driving full loaded so often that the center seat will get far more use than you might imagine.

Honda Fit

I joke that the Honda Fit is really a Honda Prius because the body styling is so similar, though it lacks Toyota's electronic sophistication. I personally know two ride share drivers driving the Fit and it works great for them. It's solid and reliable, has a cavernous interior and easily passed my personal backseat testing. The price is very similar to the Prius and the Fit ranks nearly as high both in owner satisfaction and cost of ownership.

To me the Fit and Prius are tied for the best entry level ride share car.

Mazda CX-5 and Mazda 3

I looked at various models of Mazdas but the seats in the CX-5 were kind of funky the way they were arranged. Officially the CX-5 only seats five, the same as the Prius and Fit. There just wasn't any compelling reason to work with the odd interior design. If the CX-5 seated seven and you could take XL pings, then that car would have moved to the top of my shopping list.

I also found that Mazdas as a whole lacked the "bells and whistles" of a navigation system, backup camera and entertainment system.

Again, if you already have a four door Mazda, use that.

Nissan Pathfinder

Surprisingly, the Pathfinder is on the short list almost everywhere for U and L. Since the Pathfinder seats 7, it qualifies for XL service. The gas mileage is rated at 27 highway and 20 in town, about half of the Prius and Fit. It is definitely roomy inside. I've seen entire families in Bangladesh living in smaller apartments.

The downsides are cost and gas mileage. Even used Pathfinders in decent shape are fairly spendy for a ride share car. Used Pathfinders in this area with mileage under 50K are running from $18,000 for the base models up to $25,000 for a lightly used Platinum model. The Platinum model is nice because it has leather seats. New models run from the mid-$30,000 range to the low-$40,000s.

I also see a lot of Pathfinder XL drivers taking X pings when it's slow. Generally people only call XL vehicles when they have a large party because of the higher cost. Consequently, you'll be running full most of the time on XL calls. Just like at every service level riders will still try to get more people into your car than it is legally rated to carry. I have seen, with my own eyes, U drivers smiling while eight or nine people piled into their SUV rated for seven passengers. That is taking a huge liability risk and it encourages passengers to keep trying to game the system.

Gas mileage is a factor unless you believe gas is going to stay at $2/gallon for years to come. I don't, and that's the primary reason I went with the lowest tier service and the car with the highest gas mileage.

If you live in a place with a lively entertainment district, some U drivers do quite well driving XL, especially on the weekend. If you're thinking of just driving during events and  conventions, then an XL vehicle, which includes most SUVs and minivans, is the way to go.

It should be noted that Consumer Reports names the Pathfinder as one of the seven cars owners regret buying.

My Choice

I went with the Prius V, which is the wagon. It's the only Prius model that didn't have a pronounced slope to the back and it's roomy enough inside to play racquetball. It's also got a massive cargo area, big enough for luggage for three to four people going on a long trip. The back seats are adjustable, both front to back and tilt. The middle seat is also comfortable, even though the seatbelt for the middle seat is oddly placed. I routinely get compliments from passengers about how roomy and comfortable it is in the backseat.

Like most new Toyotas my Prius has a wireless key that you don't have to take out of your pocket to start the car. Once you get used to that it's hard to go back to fumbling with keys. It also comes standard with an entertainment system that is Bluetooth enabled, a backup camera (you really want a backup camera) and a large assortment of strategically placed cup holders.

There are quirks that take some getting used to in the Prius Hybrid, like the engine shutting off when the battery is charged. That can be dangerous if you think the car has stopped and take your foot off the brake. The shifter and wiper controls are so close to one another that I have hit one reaching for the other. It's also got a crazy loud backup alarm. The alarm doesn't warn people outside you're backing up, it blares inside to remind the driver that the car is in reverse and not drive. The reverse warning alarm is really shrill and like stabbing an ice pick into your brain over and over.

Another potentially dangerous issue with the Prius is the continuous power transmission. It's great for gas mileage but on hills it will start to roll backwards if you take your foot off the brake. A lot of the hotels here have ramps and I almost rolled back into a passenger I didn't realize was part of a group getting in the car. Now I keep it in park until I'm sure everyone is inside.

I almost ruled that car out because of the color, which is red. I personally don't like red, then my wife pointed out she liked it and it was easier to see. Visibility is a big issue and, since roughly 60% of my customers were women, her opinion cemented the final decision. I dubbed it the Raspberry Go-Kart and, after writing a check for nearly $20,000, I was ready for business.

Making a Final Choice

Whatever vehicle you select will have to pass an annual safety inspection and you'll have to take a picture of the form and send it to U and L. Since you have to do that anyway, why not make sure it's going to pass before you buy it?

Download the inspection form and see if the vehicle passes. If it needs work to pass, you'll have a bargaining chip with the seller. It cost me $21 for the inspection and that's cheap insurance when buying a used car.

Debt

What I can state with absolute conviction is that **going into debt for a ride share car is one of the worst financial decisions you can ever make.** Whether that debt is in the form of a lease or a loan, just don't do it. If you're depending on income from ride sharing, that payment is going to drag on your finances like an anchor. Find the best car you can afford to pay cash to secure and drive it until it dies. When you're absolutely sure it's dead, pull the tags and have it towed to the scrap yard. If you're going to lease a car, you should make sure it's big enough to sleep in.

Final Thoughts On Cars

Ride share drivers are using a bewildering array of vehicles. Besides the models listed above, I looked at Kia, Hyundai and virtually every car brand on the market. If it's got 4 doors and is in cosmetically decent shape and newer than 10 years old, you'll likely be able to use it. I made the choice I did for a lot of reasons other than the ride share business. Had this car choice been focused exclusively on ride share driving, I would have opted for a less expensive car with more miles.

For most of you the car you'll start with is the one you already have.

ACCESSORIES – OUTFITTING YOUR CAR

Having a car is only the first step in your ride share experience, now you have to set it up for ride share driving. That means making a few changes to make your car interior more welcoming for customers and safer for you. Many of these items I figured out on my own, others were suggestions from other drivers.

Some of these suggestions will vary by region. For Instance, here in Florida I don't need tire chains or floor mats that can provide protection from slushy boots or an ice scraper for the windows. On the flip side you may not need a blanket for wet swimsuits and oily sunscreen on people who've been out on the beach all day. Yeah, I know, life's tough here in the tropics. The fact is every place has a few pieces of unique gear specific to that area.

The number one accessory that should be the first thing you purchase for your car is universal.

Don't take your car out of the driveway

without a dash cam. Get one that has an interior camera besides showing the road in front of you. If there's ever a dispute about your passenger's behavior or your conduct as a driver, the dash cam footage will be your salvation. Make sure to check out the legalities of video recording in your state.

This is the camera I picked. The cord for the rear camera was too long, so I got a shorter cord with the same type connectors and mounted the rear camera next to the mirror so it covers what's going on inside the car. That way the video shows both what's happening inside and outside the car. The video wasn't great at night but I'll show you how I fixed that later and made the car interior more inviting for customers at the same time.

This Falcon Zero is a popular choice among ride share drivers, giving you a nearly circular field of view. It's also more portable if you need to move it between different vehicles. An extra bonus is the Falcon Zero has night vision for better interior video at night. In hindsight, I'd probably spend the extra money for the Falcon Zero if I were at all confident in my ride share future.

One thing that really sticks with customers are drivers who don't have their phone mounted in a way that's easily visible with both hands on the wheel. You'll get down-rated by customers for looking down at your phone, called Chimping. The most common type of phone mounts have some type of suction device to attach them to the windshield. Those work in a lot of cars but the windshield slopes too much on a Prius and the suction mounts left the phone awkwardly far away.

Then I tried the type that fits in the cigarette lighter. The problem with those is the arm is so long that the phone wobbles and I still had to look down to see where I was going. That was no good and the lever arm put too much torque on the 12 volt port.

After experimenting with different types of phone mounts, I finally settled on one that was, perhaps ironically, the least expensive one I tried. It was also the last one I tried. It's just a fairly basic air vent mount. I use the bottom vent so the weight of the mount is resting on the vent bottom and not the vent fin itself. It keeps the phone below my view of the road but high enough I don't have to look down to watch the GPS map.

This suggestion came from fellow driver SteveK2016 in Atlanta. I got a set of LED interior lights that mount under the seats. It took about an hour to install them and then download the free controller app.

At night nearly every customer getting in the car complimented the lighting. The added visibility is also a good thing. With the right interior lighting you can see what your passengers are doing in the backseat. That will be more important than you might imagine. It also provides enough light for the dash cam interior camera. The only downside to the lights is they show every speck of dirt on the floor. That means I have to vacuum more than normal but it's totally worth it.

A Good Flashlight

A good flashlight is essential for several reasons. It's vital in an emergency and useful for lighting up hard to read house numbers on dark streets. I choose the Sabre S-2000SF with several unique features. It's rechargeable, so I don't have to mess with batteries. It's compact enough to clip inside my pocket and it's made of aircraft aluminum and can be used as a striking weapon. Besides the flashlight it's got a switch setting that turns it into a powerful stun gun.

Again, you should know your state's rules on stun guns before adding one to your kit. Only once did I think I'd have to use that feature. Both U and L define what they consider a "weapon" and it's unclear where stun guns fit in the definition.

A Tip Sign

The subject of tip signs is covered in more detail in later chapters. After a lot of experimentation I eventually decided to just to leave mine up.

Chargers Cords and Connectors

I had every kind of phone charger imaginable and a heavy duty 12 volt cord with a USB connector. It was a waste of money. The only cord ever used was the AUX cord and you'll get tired of people taking over your entertainment system real fast. I made a USB power port available for anyone with their own charge cord but that was it.

A Dog Blanket

You can't refuse to take passengers with service dogs and dog owners are thrilled when drivers let them bring their pets. I got the type that hangs from the headrests and the bonus is it's waterproof which  makes it perfect for resort areas when people might have wet swimsuits or be sweaty from running.

It takes a minute to install and take out but it's worth it. I'll give the riders the option to cancel and call another car if they're in a hurry but that's never been a problem.

Seat Covers

I used the dog cover in lieu of seat covers. Honestly, I was going to get seat covers, just never got around to getting them ordered. Most drivers like a type of fabric called leatherette because it's less absorbent. At a minimum invest in a can of ScotchGard. I almost got burned putting that off, so don't make that mistake.  Dash cam and seat covers are 1 and 2 on your accessories list, in that order.

Emesis Bags

I learned about these training as an EMS on the fire department. They're bags with a hard plastic collar, slightly funnel shaped, for people getting sick. They fold nearly flat and are quick to deploy if someone gets queasy. Best of all they're really inexpensive. They're much better for containing an accident than trying to get the smell out of your upholstery.

Cleaning Supplies

Go to a pet store and see if they carry a product called Nature's Miracle for pet accidents. That stuff is like magic on stains and smells. Another product to carry that every boat captain on the planet swears by is Simple Green, but test that before using it on seats or upholstery. Beware of products containing ammonia, which can contribute to deterioration of materials inside your car. I also carry glass cleaner but more on that in a minute.

Disposable Gloves

Your cleaning supplies should include disposable gloves. I get the kind I used to on the fire department and carry a pair of those in the storage under the cargo mat. If you have to do any type of cleaning, definitely wear gloves. You can get boxes of disposable gloves cheap if you have a Harbor Freight near you.

Paper Towels and a Cotton Towel

That should be obvious to carry paper towels but don't use them on windows. Paper towels have glue binding the layers together which leaves a residue on the glass. The paper towels are for cleaning and the clean cotton towel is for windows.

A Small Trash Bag

This is another obvious one. If you have to clean up a mess, you don't want it riding around in the car.

Here's what my car looks like inside with all the kit installed. The black blob right at the bottom of the frame is the USB port connected to the 12 volt extension cord.

INSURANCE

Insurance is another topic that's boring enough to make your eyes bleed and yet hugely important. With the wrong insurance you might not be covered in an accident and end up being personally responsible for damages or injuries. In the course of researching this book it should come as no surprise by now that I discovered most ride share drivers are driving with the wrong type of insurance.

The insurance products available to you are going to vary by state. Florida, where I live, happens to be one of the worst states for ride share insurance. At least at this writing there are few vendors and coverage is crazy expensive.

The reason ride share insurance is so expensive is that U and L are considered an app-based TNC, or Transportation Network Company. Almost all insurance companies consider ride share driving business use of your car and not covered under your personal auto insurance policy. When push comes to shove, that might include the time you're not even logged into the driver app! Your claim could be denied even if you haven't driven for U and L in weeks. **In many states personal auto insurance policies are specifically allowed to exclude TNC coverage.**

If this isn't complicated enough, each state may have different requirements for ride share coverage. Not all insurance companies offer ride share insurance in your state.

But Don't U and L Provide Insurance?

The answer to that question is sometimes and, again, that answer varies by state. The insurance that kicks in from both companies covers you from the time you accept a passenger to the time you drop them off. There are specific divisions to the ride share process, called Periods. As with everything else, these values change constantly.

Understanding Your Period

Period 1 - Is the time you're logged into the driver app but haven't accepted a ride. This is where most people with personal auto insurance get burned. U and L insist your personal insurance should cover this period. Many insurance companies consider Period 1 commercial use and not covered under a personal auto policy. U and L's supplied insurance only provides limited coverage during this time. Get in an accident during Period 1 with personal auto insurance and you may be in a major bind when it comes to getting your own car fixed. If you really hurt someone the personal injury and liability limits could easily be exceeded.

Period 2 - This is the time when you've been matched with a rider and are on the way to pick them up. It now appears that U may have combined the coverage limits for Period 2 and Period 3, so you're covered up to a million in liability in the event of an accident and provided a high deductible contingent comprehensive and collision protection.

Period 3 - The time when passengers are in the car. As noted above the coverage for Period 2 and Period 3 now appear to be identical.

Driving On Your Personal Auto Insurance

Personally, I think you're a fool if you're ride share driving with nothing beyond your personal auto coverage. If you lie to your insurance company out driving for a ride share company, you could definitely land in hot water. And yet, here in Florida at least, thousands of drivers are doing just that; risking a judgment and risking their car. If you're driving ride share on your personal auto insurance and you owe on your car or lease it, that's the very definition of insanity. I'm not sure what people doing that are telling themselves or thinking.

Most States Have Reasonable Options

You're lucky if you live in a state where your regular insurance company offers ride share coverage. In states with competitive options the ride share endorsement may only cost you 20%-30% more than your normal auto insurance. But, not here in Florida, at least not at this writing.

What I Paid

I have a perfect driving record, no tickets or accidents and a car I own. My perfect record ride share coverage here in Florida is $1,856.00 every six months. That breaks down to $309.33 per month for insurance. That's more than some people make on a car payment and personal auto coverage. Given what I make driving for U & L, I have to drive nearly two weeks just to cover my insurance tab. Most months I end up losing money strictly because of the insurance bill. At our South Florida rate of $0.85 a mile, that means I have to drive 475 miles, with passengers in the car, to cover my insurance.

There's no way I can keep driving, even if I wanted to, paying that insurance rate. That's competitive with what some livery drivers are paying for commercial insurance. So, I have commercial car insurance rates and still have all the limitations of a ride share endorsement. Even though I'm paying commercial rates, I'm not covered for making deliveries, so I can't even deliver pizza or U-Eats to help make ends meet.

Why Didn't I shop Around?

You think I didn't? Right now there's a shortage of companies offering coverage here in Florida. Just recently I learned State Farm may be offering a ride share endorsement in this state. Many Florida drivers are reporting similar quotes to what I paid in the driver forums. It might be possible to reduce my coverage if I carry a higher deductible and lower coverage amounts but doing so raises risk of getting sued personally. I'm just not willing to accept that level of risk. The last place you want to be in life is in between billion dollar companies arguing about which one of them is responsible for a claim. When the elephants start dancing, you're the one that gets crushed.

Drivers in other states are quoting much more reasonable rates. Therefore, I'm calculating my profit with and without the insurance coverage.

That way it's more fair for people in states with better insurance options.

The most important factor here is don't drive without a ride share endorsement and don't lie to your insurance company. You could get saddled with a judgment or expensive repair bills. It's just not worth the risk. The fact that U and L let drivers into the system with nothing but personal auto coverage demonstrates that they have no qualms about letting you take the risks.

THE RATINGS GAME

When it comes to U and L some elements of the services work well and others are dysfunctional to the point of near insanity. One of the most dysfunctional aspects to U and L are the rating systems. Overall, L is slightly less dysfunctional than U when it comes to ratings but they are both slanted against the driver.

If there's one aspect to ride share driving that will undermine your confidence as a human being and motivate you towards a new line of work, it's the driver rating system. Low ratings happen to everyone. Santa Claus could be driving ride share and someone would ding his driver rating because his sled was too breezy. It still hurts when it happens to you, especially if you're really trying to do a good job.

Not a 1 to 5 Scale

First, it's not a scale from 1 to 5 for drivers, it's a scale from 4.6 to 5. If you're driver rating slips below 4.6, you won't be driving anymore. If it falls below 4.68 you'll start getting warning notices about your driver rating.

One of the perverse aspects to driver ratings is how few low marks it takes to get into trouble, especially if you're new. Ratings are averages of your rating over 500 rides, which may soon include a secondary rating of the last 100 rides. A smaller number of data points will mean poor ratings drop out sooner but it also means they count for more in the short term. Like any average that number is highly variable with a small data set. I had one couple from New York...and I will never forget you two...who lowered my score from 4.96 to 4.84. They could do that damage, with a pair of 2-star ratings, because I was a nice guy and didn't want to strand them in a bad part of town. Lesson learned there. Now I'd let the pimps and drug dealers boil them in oil before letting them in my car again. If an L passenger rates a driver poorly, they won't be matched up again in the future.

The perverse and hair trigger rating system means it's better to let your cancellation and acceptance rates take a hit before you allow a passenger in your car who's going to give you a bad rating.

The Golden Rule

The golden rule for ride share driving is **no passenger can rate you until after you start the trip**. That means don't start the trip until you're ready to go. Just because you accepted the ride request doesn't mean you have accept the rider. Remember that riders don't have access to the rating screen unless you start the trip!

If you don't like the looks of the person or party, cancel and drive away. That means you have to assess the passenger before he or she gets into the car. Which brings us to the second rule of safeguarding your driver rating.

Keep The Doors Locked Until You're Sure

Getting in a hurry is your biggest enemy. You want to take a moment to look over your passengers before letting them in the car. I usually parked a little ways from the door so I have time to watch them approaching the vehicle. The most obvious thing you're looking for is open containers of alcohol or any drinks in a container without a lid. I'm constantly amazed that people who would never think about eating or drinking in a friend's car have no compunction about messing up a ride share vehicle.

Don't Open The Doors Until The Entire Party Is There

I always ask if this is the entire party before opening the door. The reason for that is it's easier to keep people out of the car than chase them out. Passengers are clever, they know some drivers actually enforce the rules and some of them get sneaky about trying to bring drugs or alcohol on board. In my experience it was always the stragglers bringing the problem. If the rest of the party is already in the car that's going to make your situation that much more difficult.

The penalty for cancelling is better than the penalty for a low driver rating. It's better to tell them no and drive away than tell them no after you start the trip and your driver rating is on the line.

It's Not An Equitable System

In the early days ratings mattered for riders as much as drivers but that's not the case today. Most passengers don't even realize they have a rating and the company is much more willing to remove a bad rating from a passenger than a driver. As U and L try to become a mass transportation system and push further down the rider food chain, there are more undesirable riders. The perversity of the rating system gives these low-end riders a monstrous sense of entitlement that comes through in how they treat drivers. If passengers got deactivated when they're rating slipped below 4.6, you'd see a lot better behavior in the car. After they've been booted from both ride share applications their only option would be the cab and cab drivers will be happy to put up with their attitude for $3.00 a mile.

Protect Yourself

When it comes to ratings, there's no margin in being nice. You didn't design the rating system, you just have to live with it. A bad rating is better than a fine or having your car impounded because one of your passengers is carrying drugs. As a private vehicle you are afforded none of the protections of a commercial vehicle. I would like to think that law enforcement would be decent enough to understand it wasn't the driver's fault but you're betting your car on that decency. It's just not worth the risk.

FACTORS IMPACTING INCOME

Some of the factors impacting your income are things you can control and some are not. Before we dive into the numbers, here are the most significant factors that will influence how much you can make.

Population Density

Drivers in major cities make more and there are several reasons for that. Cities like New York, L.A., Boston, Miami and San Francisco all have very high population densities. A higher number of potential customers in a given area is definitely good news for  your income. The reason population density is so important is that it cuts down the distance between pickups. Cutting the distance cuts the time required to get there. The faster you can move passengers in and out of your car, the more money you can make.

There's actually a list of cities by population density. Going by those numbers you can see around the New York City area the population density is actually significantly higher in some cities in New Jersey. Surprisingly, New York is number 6 on the list! The numbers are the population per square mile and you can see that some cities in New Jersey are twice as crowded as New York City!

1   Guttenberg   New Jersey   57,116.0
2   Union City   New Jersey   51,810.1
3   West New York   New Jersey   49,362.4
4   Hoboken   New Jersey   39,066.4
5   Kaser   New York   27,788.2
6   New York City   New York   27,016.3

So now let's compare those figures to another major city, like Miami.

12   North Bay Village   Miami   Florida   21,484

14   Sunny Isles Beach   Miami   Florida   20,518.9

Okay, here we see that North Bay (at the northern end of Miami Beach) and Sunny Isles are the most crowded parts of Miami and that reflects the reality on the ground. During the season there is frequent surge pricing in and around Miami Beach (the bit that's out on the strip of land on the ocean side). According to the Miami numbers you'll be working in nearly the same population density as driver in New York City.

Population density means more customers looking for rides at any one time and a shorter distance between them. Now let's look at the population density where I live which is near

West Palm Beach, Florida, using 2014 numbers with the value as the population per square mile.

West Palm Beach Florida 1,833.8

Wow, compare that to Miami and New York! With a population density that low, you'd expect earnings to be lower and that's exactly how it works out on the ground. There are fewer people looking for rides and it can be a 10 to 15 minute drive to a pickup. And the population density is seasonal here, so it basically turns into a ghost town in the summer.

Let's compare that to Seattle.

Seattle Washington 6,717.0

Using that comparison, you could expect drivers in Seattle to make more than drivers here in West Palm and that comparison holds up. Population density and income is not a perfect relationship but it is a good guideline.

I realize that all this blabber about population density must seem disconnected from the topic of income but I assure you that it's one of the keys to understanding how much you can make. I will share with you how much I can make here and you can look up the population density where you live and you'll have a fair idea of your upper income.

The rate per mile that U pays you varies from city to city and between service levels. This is another big reason income estimates you see online can vary so widely. Let's compare some U-X rates for different cities. In most cases, the pricing for a major metropolitan area also includes the surrounding cities and suburbs. Please note these numbers change frequently!

Memphis

Base Fare: $0.70

Per Minute: $0.11
Per Mile: $0.80
Cancellation Fee: $5
Service Fees: $1.90
Minimum Fare: $5.85

Miami

Base Fare: $0.95
Per Minute: $0.13
Per Mile: $0.85
Cancellation Fee: $5
Service Fees: $1.70
Minimum Fare: $5

Newark

Base Fare: $1.05
Per Minute: $0.15
Per Mile: $0.87
Cancellation Fee: $5
Service Fees: $1.60
Minimum Fare: $6.55

Seattle

Base Fare: $1.35
Per Minute: $0.24
Per Mile: $1.35
Cancellation Fee: $5
Service Fees: $1.30
Minimum Fare: $4.80

Okay, these numbers don't mean a lot to you right now but soon I'll show you how those rate cards, your city's population density and your navigational ability all combine into an earnings number.

Even if you don't understand them fully, you can see the rates are vastly different between cities. The difference in pricing is influenced by the market and sometimes local laws. Looking at these numbers and the population densities, we can now make some rough comparative estimates. Drivers in Seattle should make more than drivers in West Palm (true) and drivers in Memphis (pop density 2,000/sq mi) would make the least of all (also true). Those common sense conclusions are mostly accurate but that's not the whole story. Seattle pays more per mile, per minute and the base fare is higher but the population density is about one-fourth what it is in Miami. So, you're getting paid less in Miami, but you have more customers looking for rides, especially during the season. That's where population density comes into play for your earnings!

There is a limit to how much population density helps. Your car has a limited capacity and the realities of getting from one pickup to the next limit the number of rides you can squeeze into an hour. When you're going from one ride to the next, excess population density is no longer a benefit.

Where you get clobbered as a U driver, besides living in Memphis, is if you're in a suburban area with a low population density. You're getting the rates of the nearby major city but you're working in an area with a much lower population density. A lower population density means it's more distance (and hence time) between rides and there are fewer people looking for rides (more dead time). If it's 8 minutes to a pickup and your rider takes 2 minutes to get out the door, that's one-sixth of an hour that you don't get paid for, called dead time. Now imagine you drop someone off and it's 2 minutes to the next pickup and 30 seconds for the passenger to get in the car. You just gained an extra 7.5 minutes. That's time for a new ping, travel to the pickup point and a new passenger (and base fare) in the car. You get paid for a whole new ride in the time it takes me in unpaid time to get to my next passenger and that's on a busy night! That's the difference between urban centers and suburban areas.

If the system was fair, suburban riders would pay more than people in the city. Instead, U and L punish drivers for working the burbs and low population areas. Ah, but even that's not the whole story as we'll see in later chapters.

Length of the Ride

Where suburban drivers can make up a little earnings ground is on long rides. Long rides get you closer to the theoretical maximum you can make in a hour (we have not covered the theoretical maximum topic yet). Even if you live in a suburban or low-density area, you can improve your income if you have a steady supply of riders traveling long distances, which I define as greater than 20 miles. We'll cover this topic in detail a little further down the road (you might as well get used to driving puns, too).

The ride length is important because some drivers are working toward their driver bonus or guaranteed income. With U and L you get an extra cash bonus if you get so many riders in a week, that number varies with the city, but usually somewhere between 75 and 120 rides. You have to drive a LOT to get that many people in the car and long trips, while they pay more, make it harder to get to those bonus numbers. That's why many drivers started calling ahead and canceling on long rides, because they're playing the bonus game. If you're not driving full-time, then you'll never come close to collecting a driver bonus, so your strategy will default to finding longer trips.

Surge Pricing

Another way to boost your earnings are with surge pricing. Surge pricing is when there are more customers looking for rides than there are cars available. The ride share companies send passengers a notice that it will cost them up to five or six times as much for a ride during times of peak demand and you, as the driver, make more. Most passengers will say "screw that" and simply wait until the surge pricing goes away when demand goes down...exactly what the ride share company wants them to do. A few people just bite the bullet and pay more and those rides are golden. We'll spend a lot of time on the surge in later chapters.

Driver Density

How many rides you get depends on your population density, the level of demand and the number of cars available. Ride share companies are notorious for making sure there's an oversupply of drivers. Your well-being is not their concern. Their concern is to the customers and speedy service. That's one of reasons I see the ride share industry starting to decay, but more on that later. It doesn't matter how heavy the population density, if there are five other drivers parked around you, you're not going to make any money.

Driver density is not a factor you can control but in the chapter on Optimization Strategies, we'll cover how to position yourself to be more competitive. I could simply ask U and L about driver density but they wouldn't tell me and, honestly, they couldn't tell me. All they know is how many drivers are on the app at a given time. Sometimes there will be a lot of drivers, other times very few. U and L can't tell drivers to go online because, if they start doing that, the drivers are no longer contractors, they would be employees subject to minimum wage laws and eligible for unemployment compensation.

Navigation Ability

This is a big one. The better you know how to navigate an area, the more money you can make. I've had people in the car 3 and 4 extra minutes because I missed a turn or a driveway entrance. In a business where minutes count, GPS systems are notorious for taking you out of your way. One of the biggest "features" that makes me want to bang my head on the steering wheel are when GPS systems want you take you on a three block, three-turn excursion when all you needed to do was make a U-turn. That's because U-turns aren't legal in all states and they can be somewhat dangerous. Mapping companies don't want to get sued for encouraging dangerous behaviors. So, that explains why the GPS system wants to run me all the way out to Lost Tree Village on Singer Island from North Palm Beach when all I needed to do was make a safe and, at least in this state, completely legal U-turn.

When GPS works it's magic but the unfortunate reality is it doesn't always work and it will be a long time before it can replace the spatial recognition abilities of even an average driver. Familiarize yourself with the areas you're most likely to drive by breaking them down into subsections and grids (just like in the military) and then use GPS for what it does best, zeroing in on the destination address, what I call the last mile.

Learn the major north-south and east-west roads and use those to create your city grid. Then work up a list of the highest rated hotels, restaurants and nightclubs. All you have to know is the destination's relation and direction to the major thoroughfares. I don't know Fort Lauderdale that well but I know 925 Nuevo's Cubano's is south of Sunrise and east of I-95. It doesn't matter where I am, that gives me the general direction to start out. If you start out the right way, the GPS will usually lock in after a few seconds. But sit there and watch it hunt around for direction and you can almost hear your driver rating going down.

Events and Activities

If you live in a good size city and here's also a vibrant night life in that area can make a big difference in your income. Sporting events, concerts, conventions and festivals are money in the bank. Usually both major ride share companies will offer guaranteed minimums in order to attract enough drivers to the area. Guaranteed minimums usually run from around $19 an hour to as high as $45 an hour, if you meet all the guidelines. Guaranteed minimums are specific to the city and event, there is no set pricing. The driver app will send you a notice when an event is upcoming. Events will be part of our Optimization Strategy when it comes to making money.

Your Service Level

This is a big one but it's also a big question mark. The same theory and base calculations will apply to earnings but it will be difficult to figure out how much you'll be making. The ambiguity stems from the fact you can't always tell how much you'll be working at any particular service level. Sure, you'll make more driving a luxury SUV. Unfortunately, you'll work less often and spend more time waiting around. In the meantime you'll be paying for insurance, gas, and maintenance on a $65,000 SUV. I would argue that the more exclusive service levels are for people with more experience in the car-for-hire industry. You may not want your Cadillac Escalade exclusively in service for a ride share company.

Okay, those are the major factors influencing your income in the ride share business. Now we can start looking at some actual numbers (finally!) and how all those factors combine into an answer to the question of how much you can make.

THE MODEL RIDE & THEORETICAL MAXIMUM

The first pass at figuring out how much you could realistically make driving for a ride share company and back-checking the outrageous income claims you sometimes read in driver forums and Craigslist starts by creating a standard I call the Model Ride. With nothing more than a rate card and calculator, you can do a quick calculation of an average non-surge ride. Basically what we're going to do is create an earnings model for non-surge driving, called the Theoretical Maximum, and that starts with a basic ride model.

The Theoretical Maximum is the amount of money you could make in a perfect ride share environment going by the published rate cards. That's with zero time and zero miles between passengers all going on perfect 20 minute trips that are exactly the same time and exactly the same distance. Later, we'll use actual trip data to refine our model.

Step one is getting rate information for our model ride. Start by looking up the rate card for your area. That site also has some excellent aggregate numbers for rates. Where I live Miami's numbers apply. You can follow along with the numbers for your city. If your city isn't listed you can always contact the companies directly to get the rate card for a specific area.

Miami

  Base Fare: $0.95
  Per Minute: $0.13
  Per Mile: $0.85
  Cancellation Fee: $5
  Service Fees: $1.70
  Minimum Fare: $5

So, let's take our theoretically perfect 20 minute trip at 25 mph. Why 25? Because that's a fairly good average speed for driving in a mixed urban/suburban area. If you want to get really technical there are websites that track average driving speeds for major areas. For now we'll use 25 mph and use that to calculate the distance:

20 minutes at 25 mph is going to be roughly 8.3 miles.

So, now we have a distance and a time and we can solve for the cost of that ride:

base fare $0.95 + (20 minutes x $0.13) + (8.3 miles x $0.85) =

$0.95 + $2.60 + $7.05 = $10.60

Before we go any further, let's look at a real world drive of roughly the same time and distance and see how our theoretical compares with the reality.

11/25/2016 u-x 7.91 (miles)   24 (minutes) = $10.88 (total fare)

Not bad, right? The distance is a little off and the time is a little off but our model ride is right in the ballpark.

Now we can say that in a perfect world, with zero time between customers and no dead time, you could fit 3 identical rides in every hour.

$10.60 x 3 = $31.80

In our theoretically perfect ride share world, your absolute maximum earnings are roughly $30 an hour (I'm rounding for easier calculations).

Right, so we're throwing around some numbers like $30 an hour and you're probably getting excited. Don't get too worked up, all we've done is calculate an absolute fixed theoretical limit. Physicists can calculate the speed of light but that doesn't mean we're getting there anytime soon. The reality is going to lower that number quite a bit.

First off, U and L both take a cut of those theoretical earnings. The companies actually take two cuts; one that you see and one that you don't. What you don't see is that both companies are also taking a booking fee, also called a service feel, right off the top; that comes off before you see the fare.

A Quick Word About The Service Fee

For my numbers I took U and L's face value fare and calculated their cut without adding the service fee back in. The company takes an additional 25% after the service fee. I'm using 25% because I don't see the point of adding the service fee (also called a booking fee) back in when doing the calculations. If I added it back to the fare, I'd also have to add it to the U and L fees. So, what you actually get paid would come out exactly the same. You're getting paid the rate card regardless of what the passenger is paying. U & L are both subsidizing the cost of rides but that doesn't concern you as a driver, that's between the passenger and the company.

I'm trying to show what you can make driving and treating the booking fee like a constant. Just understand that it's there but you don't see it.

This infographic from The Ride share Guy explains, in mind-numbing detail, how the service fee changes the percentages U and L get if you really want to see those numbers. It also covers the impact of rate cuts in the same graphic, which is a bit confusing. In an effort to keep our calculations simple, I'm not going that far down in the weeds.

I'm ignoring the service fee for most of the theoretical calculations because it's taken out before you see the fare. What you make is what you see on the ride data and I'm shaping my models to reflect what you'll actually bring home.

Back To The Model

Let's go back to our original theoretical ride and take out the company's cut.

$10.60 x 25% = $2.65 (company percentage)

$10.60 - $2.65 = $7.95 (projected earnings)

Now let's check that against our real world

ride once again with the company cut taken out.

$10.88 (total fare) - $2.72 (U percentage) = $8.16 (actual payout)

Our model ride is holding up pretty well to a ride that's roughly similar in time and distance.

The company percentage alone cuts your theoretical maximum hourly earnings from $31.80 to $23.85. In other words, in an absolutely perfect trip world, you're maxed out at under $24 an hour using Miami rates.

Now we can back check our earnings numbers by checking the actual ride against our projected hourly earnings.

60/24 minutes = 2.5 (the number of times 24 goes into 60)

$8.16 x 2.5 = $20.40 hourly rate

Comparing the actual road-driven numbers to our theoretical calculation of $23.85 and, once again, we're very close.

The model and reality line up pretty well. This is the crude calculation which we'll continue to refine. The difference in the numbers is likely due to minor variations in real world driving. That's okay because our model is within a couple dollars and already is a powerful tool to help spot company trolls in public forums and untrue statements in the media.

What we're ignoring right now are circumstances when you get paid more than the Theoretical Maximum. Surge pricing, guaranteed minimums, bonuses, events and tips are all factors that can increase your earnings. We'll talk more about ways to beat the Theoretical Maximum in the chapter called Optimization Strategies. We're also ignoring expenses, slow days and other factors that reduce income right now, which come out of your share.

You can see by now how the Model Ride helps calculate the Theoretical Maximum. It sets an absolute, fixed and outside limit on how much you can make under perfect circumstances. Most of you are smart enough to know that circumstances are never going to be perfect and that's what we're going to cover in the next section. I'm going to show you how to take that theoretical maximum and whittle it down to a number that's actually pretty close to reality.

But already you have a powerful tool for taking a ballpark guess at how much an average ride pays. Let's try another city like Dallas, TX. Here's the U-X rate card for Dallas:

Base Fare: $1
Per Minute: $0.10
Per Mile: $0.85
Cancellation Fee: $5
Service Fees: $1.70

Just like up above, we use our 20 minute, 8.3 mile estimate to baseline hourly earnings:

Base Fare ($1.00) + time (20 min x $0.10) + miles (8.3 miles x $0.85)

$1.00 + $2.00 + $7.05 = $10.05

Now take U & L's cut: $10.05 x 0.25 = $2.51

Your payout then is $7.54

Multiply that times three and the Theoretical Maximum in Dallas is around $22/hour driving classic U-X during non-surge times.

Okay, once more with the Seattle rate card:

Base Fare: $1.35
Per Minute: $0.24
Per Mile: $1.35

Cancellation Fee: $5
Service Fees: $1.65

Create the model ride.

$1.35 + (20 min x $0.24) + (8.3 x $1.35) = $17.35

Take out U's service fee: $17.35 - 25% = $13.01 (estimated)

Now let's compare with an actual ride I got from a Seattle driver:

Seattle U-X 9/23

Fare $15.23

U-Fee -$3.81

Duration 17 Min

Distance 7.14

$15.23 - $3.81 = $11.42 (actual ride)

You can account for the difference with lower mileage but how nice our model is working! Interesting to see how the exact same ride pays substantially more in Seattle than it does in Dallas. Now you can calculate a model standard fare for almost anywhere by just getting the rate card and following along with one of these examples.

The Pool Factor

But you won't make $23/hour, even if you drive X perfectly because, eventually, you'll get pulled into the Pool. U-Pool and L-Line are the services where riders get matched up with other people going the same general direction and share the car.

U loves Pool because it's very profitable for them. Drivers hate Pool because it's more work for less money and Pool customers generally don't tip and they are driver rating killers (see chapter on Pool and Line - Welcome To Hell).

Since Pool and Line are, in fact, a rate cut for drivers. That's why the ride share companies don't widely publicize those rates. When it comes to evaluating how much you can make driving for U or L, anytime there's obscurity, it's probably working against you. The problem then becomes figuring out how the Pool variable impacts your earnings. Fortunately, just recently, U came out with a driver addendum that actually spelled out Pool rates for this area.

Miami Pool Rates

Base Fare: $0.95
Per minute: $0.10
Per mile: $0.75
Booking Fee: $1.60
Minimum Fare: $6.00
Cancellation Fee: $2.00
Rider No Show: $5.00

While $0.03 a minute less doesn't sound like much, you do a lot more sitting around in Pool because you're constantly making pickups. U thinks your waiting around time is worth $6.00/hour. It also cuts the mileage rate by $0.10 a mile and that does hurt. The only bright spot in those numbers is the $6.00 minimum fare, which will cut down on people using Pool for short trips.

You can take your calculator and make the adjustment to the model ride and see exactly how much Pool passengers will cost you.

Even that is not straightforward because not all your rides will be Pool. Not everyone wants to share the intimate confines of the backseat of your car with some random stranger who may bath at irregular intervals or hear voices telling them their fellow passengers are spying on them for the government. You also don't have to accept every ride request that comes your way and the rides experienced drivers are most likely to ignore are Pool requests.

That's a long-winded way of building up to the point, which is that, because of Pool, you'll never make the Theoretical Maximum. Pool and Line will lower your earnings. Pool and Line riders also tip far below the average for other types of passengers. Pool and Line passengers are, for the most part, bottom feeding mass transit refugees who should get back on the bus where they belong.

How many Pool and Line requests you get also varies from night to night. It really depends on how many drivers are letting those requests roll by.

We'll discuss this more in a later chapter but, for now, let's just accept that Pool will chisel still more off your Theoretical Maximum. As an X driver, unless you're really skilled and a little bit lucky, it's a rare day that you'll beat $23 an hour.

Depressed yet? Hang in there, it gets worse.

In our exploration of the theoretical we've discussed that there are ways to beat that maximum, but there are also many ways the distribution can beat you. Up to now we've been assuming zero time and zero miles between passengers. Let me tell you how often that happens...never. There's time waiting for people to get out to the car (remember, your time is only worth $0.13 a minute, so what's the rush?), time waiting for the next ride request, passengers who want you to wait while they run an errand and time to get to the next pickup. There are also times you just won't like the passenger and choose to cancel them. You will never make three perfect 20 minute rides in an hour because of those factors.

This is where population density feeds back into earnings. Population density is the number of people per square mile. The more people living in a particularly area, the more people who are looking for rides. When the population density is really high, that means it's a shorter distance to the next pickup and more rides per hour. There are also more surges in urban areas, the surges last longer, more special events and guaranteed minimums. Even if you cancel a passenger here and there because they look sketchy it's only a short hop and very little time to the next ride.

Let me tell you what happens when I cancel a ride here in tropical suburbia. It took me between 8 and 12 minutes to get to the rider and figure out they're not getting in my car. So, I leave and go back online and it's probably that long to the next ride request (called a ping) and between 5 and 8 more minutes to the next pickup. If those intervals were all 10 minutes, that would be a half-hour of unpaid time and dead miles. Now you know why some drivers will go down to Miami where 10 or 20 of them will share a cheap hotel room. They're working an area with a higher population density and an urban area with fewer gated communities.

To stay organized, let's recap the things that will increase your earnings and things that will decrease them.

Increase Factors

Surges

Long trips (more miles, less dead time)

Guaranteed minimums

Driver bonuses

Tips

Decrease Factors

Pool/Line riders

Canceling an undesirable passenger

Long pickups

Extra stops

Waiting around for passengers

Now you have key pieces of information to start refining our model for earnings. With our rate card estimates in hand we can start refining based on real world numbers.

THE REAL NUMBERS

Do NOT read this chapter first. If you read these numbers out of context, you will come away with the wrong conclusion!

Before we get into this section, I need to define a couple terms. There are two ways to measure time when it comes to ride share driving. One is the actual number of hours you spent online. That's having the driver app open and being online. Then there are the actual clock hours, which encompasses when you leave the house until you get back. It also takes in any offline time for going to the bathroom, eating or pumping gas. To keep these terms clear, I'll use online hours for time online and actual hours for the total time I was out driving. In a minute it will become clear why the company wants to limit its view to Online Hours.

Using a combination of published rate cards and actual ride payments, we've established the absolute maximum you can make under perfect conditions, which don't actually exist. There are very few circumstances where you actually make that much, so your actual earnings will vary quite a lot.

Now you have convincing proof, when driving the lowest service level, that the $90,000 number the company leaked in 2014 is an absolute fantasy. $60,000 is a fantasy but one you might be able to make in some markets (but don't count on it). Even $45,000, outside of high density major markets, is nearly impossible. It does help explain why one ride share company paid a $20 million dollar fine for misstating driver earnings.

What Will Boost Those Numbers

We did overlook several factors in these numbers. Those include tips, long trips, surge pricing and guaranteed minimums. There have been days where I came very close to the theoretical maximum earnings, counting long trips and tips, and, more than once, could have exceeded it had I managed my day differently. So, yes, it's possible. Let me be clear, those days where you beat the theoretical maximum are few and far between (at least around here). Those days are also subject to confirmation bias, which is the tendency for humans to remember the good while forgetting the bad.

There Will Be Slow Days

On the flip side of that coin, there will be slow days. Let's take a look at a relatively typical Monday night working for L:

Type	Fare	Fee	Miles	Time	Hourly	Tips
L	$9.53	$2.38	7	20	$7.11	$1.00
L	$12.24	$3.06	9.9	22		
Line	$4.30	$1.08	1.9	10	$5.58	$5.87

Right now let's focus on the last column in the first row and numbers to the far right in the bottom row.

The second to the last number in that row are my earnings per hour. By my calculation I was on duty 3.5 actual hours. By L's calculation it was 2.75 (online hours). So, 3.5 hours represents my investment in time. My earnings per hour, based on that figure, are a meager $5.58 an hour and that's before expenses! Even using L's online hours only raises my hourly earnings (not counting the $1.00 tip) to $7.11/online hours.

The $1.00 at the end of the first row is the tips column. Unlike U, L has a tip screen in their app. Monday night a pair of very nice soldiers out on the town tossed me a buck. I have found that, despite the tip screen, L riders are only slightly more likely to tip than U riders and tip less when they do. Adding in my tips for the night raises my hourly earnings to...woohoo!...$5.87 an hour, before expenses. That's less than minimum wage, including tips. Take out expenses and, not only did I not make much money but added miles to my car, spent money for gas and ignored the opportunity cost of working another job during the same time.

I would like to tell you that nights like that are rare but, sadly, lower earnings are the reality on many weekdays and weekday nights. You have to be prepared for the good and the bad. The majority of drivers do not understand the economics of the business they're in and most will eventually drop out.

To be fair that Monday night was my lowest earner ever. You've already seen the population density here is relatively low and L is not well served in this area. In Miami I would certainly have made more money. That was also the Monday night before Christmas week. If there's ever going to be a night that people are saving money and not going out, it's the Monday night before leaving on vacation. The football game that night was a snoozer and I wasn't online with both services because I wanted to generate separate numbers for both U and L.

Analyzing Weekly Pay Numbers

The weekly pay numbers can be very revealing and give us another key piece of data to refine our model. Let's take a look at some weekly earnings numbers for U and measure those against our theoretical calculations. This is for the week ending December 19, 2016.

Payment Summary	Mon, Dec 12 - Mon, Dec 19
$214.86	
Total Payout	

4.8	16.47	31
Current Rating	Hours Online	Trips

As you can see by my driver rating, this was not a fun week. Other than the rating, it was a fairly typical week. First, let's look at the online hourly earnings. During that same time period I made $30 in tips (yes, IRS, I reported my tips) which means my total take was $244.86 for that week.

$244.86/16.47 = $14.86/hr (online hours, including tips)

To get that 16.47 online, I was actually out 22 hours total (remember, this was over a whole week). Now the numbers look like this:

$244.86/22 = $11.13/hr (actual hours, including tips)

That $11.13 an hour number is actually pretty consistent over time. Some higher, some lower but right around there. Remember in our theoretical calculation we were using 3 rides an hour. Now we can see the actual number of trips per hour.

31 trips divided by 16.47 clock hours = 1.88 rides per hour.

Now when you hear that baloney company claim that lowering prices attracts more riders and more riders means more money for you, keep that 1.88 number in mind. Around here 2 rides per hour is as fast as you can go. My highest ever rides per hour over a week was 2.1. It doesn't matter how many people need rides, you're only going to get two, maybe three, in the car every hour, provided one of them is either a shorter trip or a short pickup. Consequently, when you make less off those 2 or 3 rides, you make less money.

To back up that observation, let's take a look at some of my daily logs. This one is for 1-12-2017.

Date	Type	Fare	Miles	Fee	
1/12/2017	u-x	$15.11	11.62	$3.78	5:16P (first pickup)
1/12/2017	u-x	$4.64	3.15	$1.16	
1/12/2017	u-x	$21.78	18.87	$5.45	
1/12/2017	u-x	$11.25	8.63	$2.81	7:41p (last pickup)

These numbers are for a fairly typical Thursday night here. I was gone from 5:01 pm to 8:43 pm and out for 15 minutes before the first ride request and the time between the first and last trips was 2.42 hours online, my total time was 3.7 hours. Adding it all up I made:

$52.78 (fares) - $13.20 (U fees) = $39.58 or $10.69/hour (for actual hours) before expenses and no tips. For online hours it was $16.35/hour before expenses.

Now you know why the companies like to just look at clock time. You'll notice that, even with the most generous interpretation, reality still falls far short of our theoretical calculation.

We can also get the rides per hour from this night. 4 rides in 2.42 clock hours equals 1.65 rides per hour. On a long average, in this population density, with a high number of gated communities, my rides per hour works out to just under 2 rides per hour. So, this night was a little slower but fairly typical. Remember in our Theoretical Maximum, we could get three rides per hour. Now we can see how pickup times and time between ride requests play into the numbers.

If you live in a city with a high population density, with customers used to taking cabs and ride share cars, you can squeeze in more rides per hour. If you're working in the suburbs and medium size cities then 1.5 to 2.5 rides per hour is your reality.

Back To The Model

Let's take a minute and feed my rides per hour back to our theoretical model. We know that there's never going to be a perfect hour with zero time between passengers, so we know that the actual number of rides is going to be between 1.5 and 2.5 rides an hour, depending on population density. So, let's take our model ride, which is $7.95, and run a reality check at 1.88 rides per hour.

Let's go back to Model Ride and multiply by the ride per hour range.

$7.95 x 1.88 = $14.95

Now our theoretical model is getting closer to reality.

$14.95 predicted compared to $16.35 online clock hours. I beat the range because of two long rides that night but we're right in there. It's going to be hard to escape that $15/hr limit driving anywhere outside a major urban center.

You can reasonably use the range of 1.6 to 2.5 rides per hour to calculate earnings. At Miami rates, driving at non-peak times, you can expect to make between $12.72 and $19.88, not counting tips or expenses.

Now our theoretical formula is useful for estimating income. You can follow along with my calculations for where you live. Get your rate card and calculate our model ride, which is 20 minutes and 8.3 miles and work out the fare. Then multiply the fare by 0.25 and subtract that number from the original payout. Then multiply your model ride number by 1.6 and 2.5 and that will be the range for your hourly, non-surge earnings. Some nights will be higher, some lower.

Let's see how well that number stacks up against reality.

Here's another Saturday evening. This time I'm going to skip the online hours.

Date	Type	Fare	Surge	Miles	Fee	
12/10/2016	u-x	$5.31		3.67	$1.33	4:03p (time left)
12/10/2016	u-x	$3.58		2.01	$0.90	
12/10/2016	u-x	$7.38		5.56	$1.85	
12/10/2016	u-x	$8.09		5.82	$2.02	
12/10/2016	u-x	$9.28		7.19	$2.32	6:26p (time home)

2.38 hours total. $33.64 (fares) - $8.42 (U fees) = $25.22 or $10.59/hour actual time and no tips. No wonder I knocked off early that night. Notice these were shorter rides but there are more of them. I was fitting in two rides per hour but, because they were shorter trips, the actual income came out about the same. I still came very close to the range our model predicted.

I picked these days deliberately because there were no surge fares and no tips on those nights. Over a long period of time, the range of $11/hour to $15/hour, before expenses, holds up pretty well.

That $15/hour number also lines up with a Washington Post investigation (paywall). And is similar to a BusinessInsider analysis from 2014, before the second rate cut. As noted in both articles, earnings are  widely variable. That was my experience as well. There will be average nights and a few really good nights. I'll show you a few of the better ones shortly. But those good nights are not consistent enough to beat the averages. The

 averages are going to rule your experience ride share driving.

But I'm getting ahead of myself. First we need to look at those numbers figuring insurance and gas. Then we can start looking at surges and other ways that boost earnings.

FIGURING IN EXPENSES

Since we've already done the numbers we'll keep using the weekly pay numbers from the week of 19th that we used previously. Now we can do some expense calculations, starting with insurance.

My insurance tab was $1,856 for six months, which is roughly 180 days so my insurance is $10.31 a day. Going by typical days, I have to drive an hour just to pay for that day's insurance. But, since I didn't drive every day, my ride share experience was an overall money loser just because of insurance. Fortunately, you may live in a state where you have better options for ride share coverage.

To make a fair calculation I should also account for the fact I would have to carry insurance anyway. The quote for full coverage, with no ride share endorsement, was $805 every six months for similar mileage, or $4.47 per day. Therefore, my daily ride share insurance cost was actually $5.84 per day or $40.88 per week.

What I would have paid anyway: $4.47

What I paid for ride share coverage: $10.31

My actual ride share insurance cost: $5.84 per day or $40.88 per week.

You can take what you're paying now and calculate the difference with a ride share endorsement. For my case, I'll use $40.88 per week.

Let's go back up to the pay stub for the week ending on the 19th, plus tips, was $244.86. Now, deducting the adjusted insurance of $40.88, which is the cost beyond what I'd normally pay, yields $203.98. Now earnings per clock hour, which were $14.86/hour are now $11.29/hour and $9.27/hour actual time. And we still have gas to go!

These numbers explain why so many take the risk of driving for a ride share company carrying nothing but personal auto coverage. Those expenses fairly brutalized our earnings and that was after adjusting for the insurance I'd have to carry anyway!

Gas

To make it fair, I would stop at the gas station on the way home and tank up. That fill up was my gas bill for that day. What's great about a Prius is it gets unbelievably good gas mileage. Only my scooter gets better mileage and that only 10 miles/gallon more. The Prius is a wagon that holds five people gets close to the same gas mileage as my scooter! It's unreal to me how far that car can go on a gallon of gas, but I digress.

Gas receipts from 12/12/16 to 12/18/16 total $29.20. We're down to 203.98 and now we can subtract another $29.20 for gas and we get to our actual earnings minus routine expenses:

$203.98 - $29.20 = $174.78

Which is...

$10.61/clock hour (remember, this includes tips)

And

$7.94 actual hours (including tips)

Even counting tips, driving for one of the major ride share companies is basically a minimum wage job. And I wouldn't even have made minimum wage after expenses had it not been for the kindness of strangers. Keep in mind that U is still telling people it's okay not to tip.

Let's take a look a few random week pay screens and practice working the numbers. Notice the variability.

Payment Summary	Mon, Jan 16 - Mon, Jan 23

$173.11
Total Payout

4.9	16.47	33
Current Rating	Hours Online	Trips

Notice my driver rating bounced back nicely.

First, we'll add $38 in tips = $211.11

I picked this week because, bizarrely and coincidentally, it has the same number of online hours as the previous example.

$211.11 divided by 16.47 = $12.82/online hour.

I was a little better about staying online that week and managed 21 total hours (I'm rounding) to get the 16.47 online.

$211.11 divided by 21 = $10.05/actual hour

Ouch. You can see the variability already and we haven't worked expenses yet.

Minus Expenses

Minus Insurance of $40.88 = $170.23

Minus gas of $35.15 = 135.08

The Grand Totals

$135.08 divided by 16.47 = $8.20/online hours

$135.08 divided by 21 = $6.43/actual hours

Rides per hour = 2

Notice how close the rides per hour were, even on different weeks. Also, look at the difference for the exact same number of hours. Assuming I drove them both the same, or nearly the same, the difference then is distribution.

Let's look at a better week:

Payment Summary	Mon, Dec 19 - Mon, Dec 26

$309.16
Total Payout

4.9	22.75	34
Current Rating	Hours Online	Trips

Better, right? Okay, it was the week of Christmas in South Florida during a winter where it was gorgeous here and cold up north. That week was banging. The numbers:

Tips = $28

Weekly total = $337.16

Online Hourly Rate = $337.16 divided by 22.75 = $14.82/online hours

Actual Hourly Rate = $337.16 divided by 27 (rounding) = $12.49/actual hours

Minus Expenses

Minus insurance of $40.88 = 296.28

Minus gas of $34.20 = 262.08

Grand Totals

$11.52/online hours

$9.71/actual hours

Rides per hour = 1.49

One of the busiest weeks of the year and I can only manage around $10/hour.

But People Beat Those Numbers, Right?

Yes, routinely. Heck, I beat those numbers some weeks. Keep in mind those numbers are actual driving weeks, so those totals include the odd surge fare and long trips. How you beat those numbers is what we cover in Optimization Strategies. Just keep in mind, you're not going to beat them by very much and not very often.

The bottom line here is that your actual earnings are going to be much lower than you thought. U and L are both subsidizing the cost of carrying passengers and both are losing money. Both companies capitalize on driver's not being able to grasp the math of calculating their margin. Both companies dangle numbers in the media that they know are unrealistic in order to attract more drivers.

Next we need to talk about why people think they make more than they do ride share driving.

THE CLOUD OF DISINFORMATION

It's important to understand how to make rough calculations for estimating income because most people are going to seek out driver forums for advice. There is a lot of good advice there but there are also a lot of company shills.

If you do a lot of reading in driver forums, you see comments like this seeded at regular intervals:

"$100/hr is awesome. We're $55/hr weekdays and $65/ hr weekends and events."

You'll also see a ton of ads in Craigslist and other online sources, claiming you can make $1,100.00 a week or more. You should be getting wise to those claims by now.

The consistency, specificity and frequency of comments like that suggest they are being planted deliberately. Outside of major metropolitan areas, very few people in the ride share business are making anything close to that amount of money. As we've demonstrated, you can do the math rather easily yourself.

This is why you do the calculations before you get excited!

You also don't know the context. Some drivers with luxury SUVs are making decent money but their expenses are higher and they spend more time sitting around waiting. There is also a limited market for luxury SUVs during the week.

Just recently in a driver forum someone claimed he was making $1,800 a week in Salt Lake City, Utah, driving X. It's no coincidence that $1,800 a week for 50 weeks is $90,000 a year. After a while you can spot the trolls but it takes practice.

It's probably no accident that the hourly figures of $55 and $65 that you see regularly in posts, range between $110,000 and $130,000. You're probably thinking something like, "If I could make half that, I'd be doing great!" That's exactly what the company wants you to think. Dangle that kind of money in front of people and it's easy to see why they bite on becoming drivers. Some people, smart people, even leave corporate jobs to drive a ride share car. That brings us to a simple rule:

Do NOT quit your day job

Seriously, don't quit any job to drive for U or L. Believe me when I say that I totally understand the daily agony of a crappy job. But the answer to one crappy job is not jumping into another crappy job! As we'll cover shortly, you should not make a move until you're certain you understand the work and have a good estimate about how much you can make.

It wasn't always that way. In prior years, up to around the middle of 2014, you could make a living ride share driving. In some places you could make a good living. Unfortunately, that situation has changed today. Like many big companies, U and L stopped doing the things that got them to the top after they got there.

The most significant change U made that has crippled their system was cutting rates and driver pay. Before the rate cut you could make $30 an hour if you cherry picked the best times to drive. Some drivers in some cities can still cherry pick some pretty decent sideline cash but it's less common today. At that rate you could cover expenses and still make a profit. After the rate cuts drivers are starving.

My Research

I didn't just trust online sources before I started driving, I also went out and talked to people who drove for U and L as well as friends and relatives.

"A guy I know makes $500 a week," said one of my late mom's home care nurses.

"My son tried it, just to see what it was like, and he made $200 in one night," said a friend.

You too will hear stories like that and the big problem is...many of those stories are true but they tend to mask the reality rather than reveal it. The very best misinformation has elements of truth woven through it. I haven't made $200 in one night, but I've come close. That story also came with a qualification; that night was a major football game and after party in the university district and most of those rides had surge pricing tacked on. Surge times, events and guaranteed minimums can give you a skewed view of possible earnings.

When I investigated further on the claim made by my mom's nurse, it turned out those numbers were from 2014, before U slashed driver rates. Back in the day you could make that kind of money, today it's rare. And her friend drove a minivan, which qualifies for a more expensive service level and higher rates.

The Role of Confirmation Bias

What I experienced from the people I spoke with is called confirmation bias. That's the human tendency to remember the good and forget the bad. Someone goes out driving three or four times and has one good night. Does that person tell their friends the average earnings over all the nights taken together or just the highlights?

Casinos are a perfect example of confirmation bias in operation. When we talk to friends about going out for a night at the casinos inevitably someone will say, "The last time we were at XYZ Casino, Brenda won a thousand dollars!" The question that should immediately come to mind is how many times did Brenda go to that same casino and lose money? On a long enough timeline, the odds favor the casino and Brenda will walk away a loser. Confirmation bias is how some people get the skewed idea they can make a living gambling and it's a powerful force in the ride share business.

Casinos are a perfect illustration of the ride share industry. Every week in my inbox are emails from the local casino about giveaways and bonuses. Every week in my inbox were emails from U and L about weekly driver incentives and bonuses. Interesting coincidence, is it not? When you go to the casino, sometimes you have a good night and win but most of the time you'll break even or lose money. When you drive ride share, some nights you'll do really well but most nights you'll either not make much or barely break even. Both organizations count on confirmation bias to keep them in business.

I've had people tell me in driver forums that the nature of being independent means not being able to project what you're going to make. That is economic baloney. You may not be guaranteed a level of income but you should be able to estimate how much you're going to make; anything else is gambling.

Playing To Your Ego

Another consistent theme in company disinformation is the ego play. The guys who don't make money are just whiners. You can do better because you work harder and smarter. You're a tough-minded, hard-working independent businessperson. You can find an angle those less motivated people might overlook!

Like any good propaganda the ego play contains an element of truth. There are people in the U and L systems who consistently beat the averages. Some of those people are going to extremes to do it. Extremes like sleeping in their cars or having 20 to 30 people sharing cheap hotel rooms on a rotating basis.

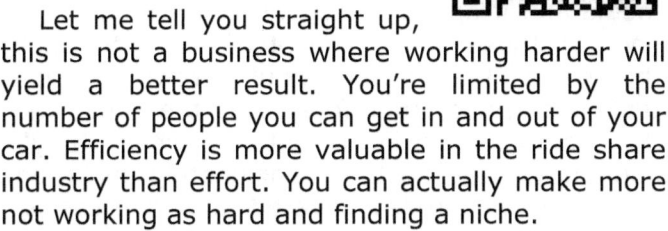

Let me tell you straight up, this is not a business where working harder will yield a better result. You're limited by the number of people you can get in and out of your car. Efficiency is more valuable in the ride share industry than effort. You can actually make more not working as hard and finding a niche.

Don't flatter yourself and don't bite on the ego play. Definitely don't sleep in your car. If you're going to invest that much of your life and gamble that large of an investment (your car), then invest that time building a sideline business that has a better chance of paying off with a living wage. There's no future in U or L as both companies are working on replacing drivers with self-driving cars.

Fielding functional self-driving taxis will take longer than the company thinks but it will come sooner than many drivers are hoping. Driving for a ride share company is a dead end job in an industry on the downslope of its lifecycle. Never forget that you are risking the value of a very expensive asset in exchange for a very small return. That's the essence of business; balancing risk and reward. Far too many people are underestimating the risks and over-valuing the reward.

Any way you cut it, driving for a ride share company is risky business.

The Big Lie - Lower Prices Equals More Income

One of the biggest talking points you see in the media is some company spokesperson saying the best thing the company can do for drivers is getting more people in cars. That's a line the company sticks to because if plays well in the media and it appeals to a particular mindset. It's one of those lines executives use to make themselves feel better about screwing people. It's no surprise, therefore, that the time when the company rolls it out is when they're announcing rate cuts. Unfortunately for them, and as we've already covered, it is depressingly easy to debunk.

As we've already seen, there's a limit to how many rides you can fit into an hour. In a high density market, you might squeeze as many as four rides into an hour, if your customers have a foot on the curb and are making short trips. Most likely the best you'll be able to do on a long average in a high density city is between two and three.

What the company is trying to suggest is that more rides will translate into more money and that's true...for the company. For you the truth is quite different. In the suburbs more rides don't help you. You're already maxed out at between two and three rides per hour, even on a busy night. Cutting the rates on your two rides per hour means you get less money for the same amount of work. More riders means the company makes more money, not you. Any increase in ridership beyond three rides an hour is little benefit to you at all.

The other angle to that statement is that they're suggesting that you're not getting more rides because there are more drivers than rides available. That would make it an example of the divide and conquer strategy. It's not the company that's the problem, it's all those other drivers taking your fares! And they suggest that as if the company has no control over how many drivers are on the road at any one time or in any particular area.

Has anyone ever gotten a message that says your area is saturated with drivers right now and you might need to wait a month or two until a space opens up? I haven't seen one. The company could easily trim the number of drivers in an area to boost the number of rides available but, somehow, that solution never makes it to the top of the pile.

That's because more rides benefits the

company and, as a side benefit, lower prices make it harder for competitors to become established or survive. U's only real competitor is barely keeping afloat. Every time U can find a way to cut rates, it makes L's survival a little more difficult.

The Referral Scam

The other reason U and L drivers may overstate earnings is to collect a referral bonus. If you give U or L a referral ID and then make it to a certain number of rides, usually 50, the person who referred you gets a bonus. Many of the cheerleaders claiming they know the secret to making more on U and L are just trying hustle referral fees. They'll even go to the bizarre length of faking pay receipts and ride screens. We'll cover the strategies to make more in the Optimization Strategies chapter but always keep in mind 1.6 to 2.5. That's as many rides as you're going to get in an hour outside major urban centers. Unless the website or ebook is selling a time machine, you'll always be up against that hard limit.

Protecting Yourself

The best protection you have from online disinformation is skepticism plus a calculator. Look up the rates for the nearest big city, run a quick calculation of our typical ride. 20 minutes and 8.3 miles, just like we covered.

Let's take one of the typical examples and use our model ride to examine it in more detail. The poster claimed to be making $1,800 a week in Salt Lake City. Let's examine that claim in light of what we've learned.

First thing you'll notice is that $1,800 a week, times 50 weeks is $90,000 a year. How convenient! Then let's look at the U-X rate card for Salt Lake City:

Base Fare: $0.45

Per Minute: $0.11

Per Mile: $0.95

Cancellation Fee: $5

Service Fees: $2

Minimum Fare: $6

As you can see just looking at the rate card, the earnings numbers are already suspicious. To make $1,800 a week is $257.14 per day, 7 days a week. You should already be able to tell that's complete nonsense. Figure two trips per hour, working 10 hours, is 20 rides. That's an average of $12.85 on each ride. 20 of those in a day, seven days in a row. In a word...no.

Even on a 7 day week, that's 270 passenger miles a day. Driving down the highway 270 miles would take you 3.86 hours. At our average speed in town of 25 mph, it would take 10.8 hours. That's 11 hours of passenger time, not 11 hours total. 11 hours of passenger time every day, seven days a week, weekdays and weekends. In science we have a word for that and that word is baloney. Most of the time you can eviscerate the trolls with nothing more than a rate card and a calculator.

POOL AND LINE – WELCOME TO HELL

If you watch the Ted Talk by the CEO and co-founder of one of the major ride share services  you'll notice that his big applause line comes when he's talking about U Pool. Pool is his whole vision for the company. Instead simply being a resource matchmaker, U is trying to drive the future of transportation. The goal is to get more people in fewer cars and replace the human drivers with robots.

In the meantime, U and L are trying to condition the riding public for that future with U Pool and L Line services. It sounds like a good idea on paper; lining up people along similar routes and letting them share a car for a reduced rate. Unfortunately, the reality is somewhat less glamorous.

Bottom Feeders

My experience with Pool and Line riders is that

they're bottom feeders who want the cheapest possible ride. Ironically, they want the discounted service but don't actually want to share the ride with anyone else. Many of my Pool riders get annoyed at going out of the way to pick up another passenger. Instead of understanding that's what they signed up for and letting the company know they're unhappy, they take out their frustration on the only person they can see...the driver. Not only are Pool riders revenue killers but they are driver rating killers as well.

Rating Killers

Inevitably, my driver ratings rose and fell with the number of Pool riders I accepted and the animosity runs both ways. Some of the lowest rated customers to ever get in my car were Pool customers. To drivers Pool and Line riders are cheapskate bottom feeders who complain when the service works like it should. Riders can sense the animosity from drivers who are either too new to know any better or are forced to take Pool pings to get their acceptance numbers back up.

Pool and Line riders also choose to remain willfully ignorant that the few pennies they get as a discount are, ultimately, coming out of the driver's pocket. As long as they can get a ride, they'll continue to cling to whatever justification they use to feel okay about taking a driver away from an otherwise productive Friday or Saturday night. The way Pool and Line are currently structured the system sets up a dysfunctional relationship between the ride share companies, drivers and riders. While services like Pool and Line may be the future of transportation, they're definitely not the present.

Awkward Silences

Pool and Line are no fun for the passengers,

either. Any conversation you were having with the first passenger comes to an abrupt halt when a ride gets matched and a stoney silence ensues. Everyone retreats to their phone and that silence becomes even more deafening waiting on a third passenger. It all combines to make a weird, awkward and no fun ride. Only inexperienced drivers take Pool rides or those who desperately need to shore up their acceptance rate. It's a dreadful experience all around and the companies should just stop trying to force them onto the market.

Recent Rider App Changes

Recent changes to the rider app make Pool the default selection in many markets. The most recent update makes switching to X an extra step. For a lot of people, who may not be good with technology, U has become Pool. In just two days I saw eight straight Pool pings and accepted only two of them and went offline instead of continuing to drive for Pool rates. Instead of cutting rates again this year, it appears U is pushing Pool, which has the same net effect as a rate cut. As far many riders can tell, Pool is the way the service works now. That will last right up until a passenger has to go out of their way and wait for some smelly person to crowd in next to them in the backseat. That's when they start asking questions about how to get a car they don't have to share.

Keep in mind U is experimenting with changes to the driver and passenger apps all the time, so this may not last.

Practice Avoidance

For a driver the problem with Pool or Line is, once you accept that first ping, you're stuck in Pool Hell. The system will start dumping passengers into your vehicle and extending the Pool drive. Almost inevitably, during times of peak demand, I had to go offline to break the Pool cycle and get back to making money. Going offline rewards the Pool customer by providing a higher level of service than they're paying for but, sometimes, that's better than letting bottom feeders keep piling into your car.

To make money as a driver then, your strategy is to minimize the number of Pool and Line riders, without getting temporarily logged off the system, which is possible. Due to the perverse nature of driver incentives, it's better to not accept a request than to accept and cancel. It's better to cancel than take a rider who's going to give you bad rating because they're not happy with the service they themselves ordered.

The Automatic Add

The problem with Pool and Line is that it ignores the ratings of the follow-on passengers after the original request. You have to look at their rating, on the way to get them, then decide whether to cancel. While you'd never accept a ping from a 3.9* rider, with Pool they're added automatically. In a system that cared about drivers, they'd let the driver set a minimum customer rating or opt out of Pool and Line all together. If U allowed drivers to easily opt out of Pool, the service would be all but dead 24 hours later and the companies know it.

Until the service finally dies or driverless cars take over the default strategy is to avoid taking Pool riders as much as possible. Thanks to changes put in place after a lawsuit judgment, at least for now U can't deactivate you for a low acceptance rate. So, you can watch those Pool pings roll by all night. The worst thing that's going to happen is you'll get logged off the system for a few minutes as a slap on the wrist. I've talked to drivers with acceptance ratings as low as 30%. If it's over 75%, you're doing something wrong. Again, keep in mind this may change in the future.

OPTIMIZATION STRATEGIES

This is the chapter where I outline strategies that will boost your earnings over the baseline average and even over the Theoretical Maximum. A couple caveats are in order. First, the same strategies don't work in every city. While many of these suggestions are location transferable, some are not or may need to be modified to fit your driving environment. Second, even if they are applicable in your city, you'll still have bad days. No system is foolproof and the distribution will kick your butt some days. There will also be other drivers also trying to maximize their income. As I've pointed out before, no matter how good the market, if you're surrounded by five other cars, you're not going to make any money.

To give you a 20,000 foot overview your optimization strategies will fall into certain broad categories:

Finding the most profitable rides
Finding the best passengers

Minimizing dead miles
Minimizing the time between rides
Keeping Pool and Line riders out of your car
Encouraging tipping (without being overbearing)

Obviously U and L are going to disagree with some of those but the numbers don't lie. Pool and Line are losers for drivers and the fewer rides you take, the higher your income.

The Most Profitable Rides

As we've seen from my ride data, the most profitable rides are long trips, which I define as 25 minutes or longer, and surge fares.

Long Trips

Even if you have to deadhead back, long trips are almost always earn more, unless they take you away from a surge area and, even then, it's worth a hard look. The problem here in South Florida is that long trips frequently take you to out of the way places that are unlikely to have any traffic coming back. For me that meant deadheading all the way back from Belle Glade (aka Sugarcanestan) one night. Here's how the math of that ride worked:

52 minutes there => total fare $40.49 => my cut $30.37

As an hourly rate that works out to about $35 an hour, which is liveable. Unfortunately, nothing comes back from Belle Glade, so I had to drive my empty car back to civilization. That means my total compensation was 104 minutes at $30.37 or $17.55 an hour before expenses. Not as good, but still more than you make on most nights driving for U or L.

So, as you can see, a long trip is more profitable, even if you have to drive back empty. Many long trip customers are cognizant that you're coming back empty and will tip you enough to at least cover your gas back. That particular customer did not tip and, surprisingly, many do not. That's because most customers going out to the sticks have been canceled on one or more times trying to find a driver who will take them. That leaves them in a less than generous mood. Even though I understand how they feel, passengers who don't tip after a long ride get a poor passenger rating from me. Getting a car as a 4* passenger will be difficult under any circumstances, no matter how far you're going. Experienced drivers with the best cars will simply let those pings roll on by. You may get a ride but your experience on the system will continue to decline and you'll have a hard time getting a car during times of peak demand.

The best long rides then are those that take you from one profitable market to another. Here that would be passengers who want to go to either Fort Lauderdale or Miami. Those trips are golden. You get the long ride, then you can either set a destination and ferry passengers back to your home court or just stay and work where you are.

Trips to Palm Beach were long and ended in a place I could work.

So, the challenge becomes where to find the best long trips that take you to a profitable area where you can work. This will be problematic if you're crossing state lines. Many times you can drop off but not solicit passengers in a neighboring state. This is a particular problem for drivers in the industrial northeast where states tend to be smaller and crossing state lines is a more frequent occurrence. Here in South Florida we have it made that way, being able to work most of the entire east coast, which is also one of the more populated areas, at least during the season.

Finding those long rides to populated markets usually starts at the airport. That's a prime watering hole when trolling for long rides to busy areas. For many airports U operates a FIFO (First In, First Out) queue. Instead of handing the call to the nearest car, U hands it to the car that's been waiting the longest. Most airports are ringed by a GPS fence and you're automatically queued inside that fence. Here the wait is frequently an hour or more. It's worth it if you get a plum ride, a loser if you don't.

Some drivers have started calling passengers to make sure a call is "worth it" before picking them up. Don't do that! Wait your turn and take your chances. When you cancel a short ride at the airport you're dumping on the next driver in the queue. There's a fine line between running your business and being a jackass.

Where long rides tend to originate:

Airports
Cruise ship ports
Convention centers
Ferry stations
Train stations
Wedding reception and party venues
Sporting events

For some of those the trick is to know where and when they begin, others when they'll be breaking up. Being profitable means knowing what's happening, when and where. Every convention center has a schedule of events. Big events should be on your schedule and make the convention center one of your "watering hole" starting points. Here in Florida knowing the cruise ship docking schedule is smart. I know tomorrow there will be a couple thousand people streaming into the port of Palm Beach and will be looking for rides once they clear Customs. I know what time the ship gets in and about how long it takes to get through the Customs line. More than a few of those calls will be long rides.

Working The Surge

When fares are surging, U and L are charging customers extra for traveling at times of peak demand. Surge fares make driving almost worthwhile and count as some of the best rides.

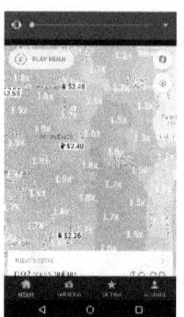
Sadly, surge rides are both elusive and rare outside major urban areas. Passengers hate surge pricing and will stand there refreshing the app until the higher prices go away. I call those people Refresh Monkeys, stabbing the refresh button over and over like monkeys in a drug addiction experiment trying to get their next fix. As a driver, scoring a surge fare can raise your hourly earnings and two or three in a row can set you up for a decent evening.

I believe, but can't prove, that the companies use "surge baiting" to lure drivers to underserved areas. How else do you explain the surge disappearing when one car arrives? If there was a heavy demand for rides, there shouldn't be any available cars.

Surge pricing can also confuse customers. A ride that costs $20 one day could easily cost $60 the next day just by leaving at a busy time. U and L could end the surge pricing by just raising rates all the time but they're not competing with cab companies, they're trying to compete with mass transit.

Like sugar on the kitchen counter attracts ants, surge pricing attracts drivers. In areas of low population density an influx of drivers can cancel out surge pricing very quickly. I suspect, but can't prove, that both companies use fake surge pricing to redistribute cars to less desirable areas. It's my belief that not all surges are real, although driver behavior could account for the sudden disappearance of surges. In the end it doesn't matter, the net result is the same.

When it comes to surge prices knowing where they're likely is more important than knowing where they are. Being in the right place when a surge starts or working areas with sustained surge pricing, which is typical at some of our nation's biggest cities, is the strategy you want to employ. L will show you the busiest times in your area.

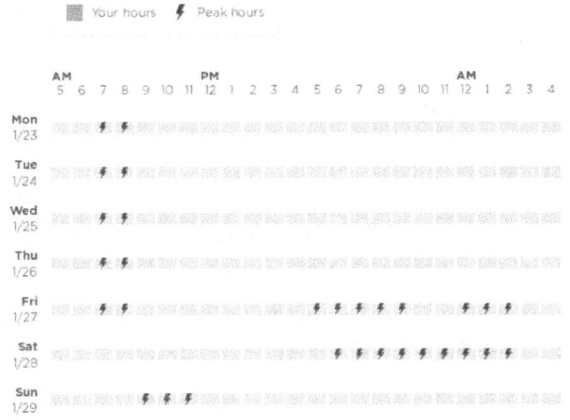

Peak time graph that's part of your L dashboard

The convenient thing about L's graph that it's a guide to the busiest times of the week and that applies to both ride share services. Think of it like your driving schedule and the times you're most likely to see surge pricing on both apps.

In my area sustained surge pricing only happens on holidays like New Year's Eve and Halloween. There is spotty surge pricing during prime time but it's usually fleeting. Many of the stories you read about drivers making hundreds a night driving usually have a surge component to them. You should not ever get the idea those nights are typical. We've already covered how to baseline what you'll make on standard fares and you should assume that will be your typical return driving.

If you live in a major urban area with a lot of surge pricing, many drivers do really well cherry picking those surge times and driving for 2 or 3 of the busiest hours. I've seen ride reports from drivers I trust showing they grossed nearly $90/clock hour on a combination of surge pricing and long trips. Of course that doesn't last but skimming the best rides and times can pay off if you're driving for extra cash.

Let's take a look at the surge on a busy Saturday night here.

Date	Type	Fare	Surge	Miles	Fee	Time
12/3/2016	u-x	$9.24		6.82	$2.31	19
12/3/2016	u-x	$3.67	$2.94	2.33	$1.65	5
12/3/2016	u-x	$15.12	$33.26	13.21	$12.10	22
12/4/2016	pool	$10.10	$3.03	10.15	$3.28	20
12/4/2016	pool	$2.15		0.99	$0.54	3

From this chart you can see why surge pricing makes such a big difference. This is a subset of my rides that night, which was a particularly busy Saturday night on into Sunday morning. I only had one other surge the rest of the night, but you can see the effect on prices. One ride went from less than $15 dollars to over $36 after fees were taken out. Now you know why drivers love the surge but there's a catch.

Non-Surge Pings During Surge Times

One of the more annoying things that happens routinely is you'll get a non-surge ping in the middle of a hot area. There are many ways that can happen.

Other drivers let the non-surge ping roll

farther and farther away.

A Refresh Monkey sees the surge disappear sooner than you do and pings a ride during the momentary break.

You make the surge disappear just arriving in the area but don't see it because of the time it takes your screen to refresh.

Passengers hate surge pricing, drivers love it. It's another one of those instances where the incentives of all the parties involved in the transaction are at odds with one another. My suggestion for both U and L would be to raise fares all the time and add a premium for rush hour and events. The premium applies despite the number of drivers in a given area. Then customers traveling between 5 pm and 7 pm know they're going to pay more. The same with bar time and events. If it cost me an extra $10 to get home after the hockey game, that's still cheaper than parking. Paying surge pricing at bar time is definitely cheaper than a DUI. Surge pricing turns what should be a routine transaction into a giant game of gotcha.

You're taking a chance letting non-surge fares roll past during surge times, but that small chance of getting timed off the app for a few minutes is often worth the risk. By practicing optimization and limiting your time behind the wheel, you can make some decent cash and then knock off before it gets ugly.

In major markets surge times can last for hours and some drivers work surge times and then go home. It's a good strategy if you can make it work. Many drivers will set surge minimums for bar time, with many refusing to go online until the surge hits 2.5 or higher. They'll also combine that will not accepting a bar time customer with a rating below 4.7. The higher rate customers are less likely to be a-hole rating killers.

Finding The Best Customers

This is harder and more subject to chance. In my experience the best customers are sober customers, although they are rarely the most profitable. Inevitably the most difficult people I deal with have been drinking and that trouble usually starts when they discover they can't bring alcohol into the car. It's hugely frustrating that more drivers don't enforce the open container prohibition. Passengers report about half of drivers let them drink in the car.

Best vs Most Profitable

I don't want to be too rough on drinkers because they're doing the responsible thing by not driving but that still doesn't make them quality passengers. They are, however, profitable passengers. Making really good money means working bar times. Do that for any length of time and you'll get people who pass out in your car, puke in your car and get belligerent with you. If someone is going to try lighting a cigarette in your car, it's going to be someone who's been out drinking.

Now you can see the wisdom behind picking the least expensive qualifying car and investing in seat covers. There's a reason cab seats look like they do. For that reason I passed on the late night crowd, except for a handful of nights so I could collect ride and surge data.

Drunks are also rating killers, much like Pool riders. You don't have to get many low ratings to be deactivated. Despite bar time surges being profitable, you may have to start skipping them or work less busy times to keep your driver rating up.

Here's my personal list of who make the best passengers:

Business people
People heading to work
Older tourists
Date night couples
Conventioneers

Business travelers were my bread and butter and I've made it my niche to find them. Not surprisingly business travelers are also U's bread and butter, with nearly 6% of all business expenses now being U related. I've discovered certain hotel chains are better than others as watering holes and I've learned their schedules. One of the Hampton Inns near here starts their buffet breakfast at 6:30 am. Usually travelers are ready to head to the job site between 7:30 and 8:00 am. Sitting outside a popular hotel will cut down on the likelihood of getting pinged by someone wanting you to run their kids to school.

Getting the best passengers also means keeping the less good ones out of your car.

! Warning - Some of these strategies below could get you deactivated. In hindsight that may turn out to be the best thing that ever happened to you but you have to decide that for yourself !

Low Rated Passengers, Pool and Line

We've already covered how Pool and Line customers tend to be the bottom feeders of the ride share industry and the riders most likely to ding your driver rating. Pool and Line riders are particularly devastating to profitable ride times because you tend to become trapped with new riders jumping in. Each new person being added means going out of your way to make a pickup and more waiting around time. All the same, letting Pool and Line pings roll by is a minor risk, particularly if you get two or three in a row. My record for turning down Pool pings is five in a row.

My strategy is to let the first one roll by, then go offline until I reach a better watering hole. Sometimes distribution gets you because most of the other experienced drivers are letting Pool requests roll by as well in a giant car version of the old card game called Shit On Your Neighbor. Pool requests roll from car to car until they get to a driver who's either new or not paying attention.

Sometimes drivers accept that Pool ping just to troll for cancelation fees. One strategy that some drivers use, that I don't necessarily endorse, is to accept the ping and just keep driving in circles until the bottom feeder gives up and cancels. Passenger cancellations don't count against your acceptance rating and sometimes you still collect a cancellation fee. Other drivers will park down the street or around the corner and then cancel the passenger as a No Show. This is a particularly attractive strategy at apartments where it's easier to hide among the other cars in the parking lot. This is how the strategy shapes up:

Don't accept the Pool request

Accept and then Cancel, which shifts the Pool ride from your Acceptance Rate to your Cancellation Rate

Accept and stall until the passenger gives up and cancels

Accept and hide until you can collect a No Show fee

The good news is the time-out on Pool rides is only two minutes, so it's pretty easy to hide long enough to collect cancellation fees.

Even practicing extreme avoidance, sometimes you just can't escape. Some drivers will pick up the first Pool passenger and then go offline to keep new riders from being added. I don't like doing that because it rewards the bottom feeder with a higher level of service than they selected. Also U sometimes updates the app and has Pool selected by default. Most customers don't pay any attention and the Pool pings flood the system until enough drivers quit or riders complain about suddenly being forced to go out of their way to share a car with one of the Great Unwashed.

Other Less Desirable Passengers

Another group of undesirable passengers to avoid are college age kids, especially spring breakers. In my experience they're the ones least likely to tip and more likely to treat your car like dorm room furniture rather than a $20,000 personal investment. Even though it's a frequent surge area, I avoid the university district here and will go offline to escape. That's ironic considering young people are some of the biggest users of ride share services. I should note that there are drivers who specialize in working the college district and sporting events and they do very well. They also have older cars with really good seat covers.

The worst customers in my book are the entitled rich kids living in gated communities. Every single one of my nightmare ride stories in this area revolve around a gated community, underage drinking, a large group of young people in various stages of inebriation and parents who are out of town. Many times they're using someone else's account or a fake name account because they get down-rated by drivers to the point where no one will pick them up. It's gotten so bad here that I just drove away and canceled at the first whiff that my ride request was a group of rich kids without an adult present. Individually they're usually fine but in groups they're almost always a problem customer.

Also on the list of undesirable passengers are parents using U and L to try and get their kids to school. Unaccompanied minors are not permitted both by insurance regulation and U's T&C. That doesn't stop busy parents from trying to use U and L as a school bus. For that reason I tended to avoid residential neighborhoods between 7:30 and 8:30 am. Usually by 8:30 school is already underway.

Minimizing Dead Miles - The Watering Hole Strategy

Dead miles and dead time are income killers. Dead miles are a triple-threat killer because they're unpaid time, you're burning gas and piling up miles on your car. Some dead time and some dead miles are unavoidable but you can minimize both of them while raising your odds of finding quality passengers by mapping out watering holes where you have higher odds of finding better rides.

Remember we talked about convention centers, train stations and popular night spots? Using a mapping app called Waze, you can create lists of your favorite watering holes and, immediately after dropping someone off, head for the nearest one. The watering hole strategy avoids the two big income killers of driving aimlessly and deadheading (driving all the way back empty). Quality watering holes also raise your chances of getting better customers.

One of my old watering holes

Another advantage is that, if you get pinged for another ride, your mapping program will automatically supersede your watering hole destination and route you directly to a paying customer, if you take the call. If it's all Pool pings, go offline until you reach your destination and then go back online where you're more likely to find premium customers.

The key to the watering hole strategy is knowing the area well enough to pick out the closest prime areas and knowing where you can safely wait for a ride.

Minimizing The Time Between Rides

There is one guaranteed way to minimize the time between rides and that's to work in areas with a high population density. If you live near a big city, you'll almost always make more by working there as opposed to the suburbs and less populated cities.

I live and drive in a land of 8-12 minute pickups and gated communities. We previously covered that when you spend 8 minutes getting to the location and 2 minutes finding your passenger, that's one-sixth of an unpaid hour gone that you'll never get back. I've had pickups as long as 22 minutes. That is one-third of an hour not only unpaid but burning gas and piling up miles on my car. Use 40 minutes in your theoretical maximum calculations to see the effect that has on your income. You'll be shocked at the result.

I've suggested to U that long pickup times, extra stops and gated communities should warrant an extra fee. Cabs make up the rate with higher per minute charges. Here our per minute fee is $0.13 a minute. That's what U and L think your time is worth.

Big cities are less likely to have private, gated streets and most of the big condo towers have a pull-over curb when waiting for guests. In my experience city dwellers are far more likely to be punctual that those in the suburbs who may utilize the service less often. The majority of the time my big city customers have a foot on the curb by the time I pull up. Those minor differences in pickup and drop off times can make a huge difference in your earnings.

Cutting down the time between rides also means avoiding another income killer, the extra stop.

Minimizing Extra Stops

The dismal per minute rate means a customer making a 6 minute stop nets you a whopping $0.78. That lost six minutes, added to the six minute pickup time, means 12 minutes of your hour gone in exchange for $0.78. No one can stay in business working for pennies.

Part of minimizing the time between customers then involves minimizing or eliminating extra stops. Since most passengers don't ask for an extra stop until you're already on the way, you're risking a 1* rating saying no. I've found that telling passengers right up front that it's busy and someone else will be waiting for the car after I drop them off. That works if it's actually busy and most of the time it's also true.

Passengers are contracting for a ride from A to B and extra stops are not part of the deal but that doesn't stop them from trying. When it's slow I try to be a little understanding but that flexibility ends during surge and peak ride times. Sometimes it also depends on the customer. In this area we have a lot of yacht crews and boat people, most of whom do not own cars. I have made stops for them during busy times because it's not like you can pull a 90 foot cruiser over to the floating cash machine in the middle of the ocean.

The best strategy for extra stops is heading them off before you start the trip. I finally had to resort to putting up a sign on the back of my headrest that said no extra stops on Friday and Saturday nights.

I gave boat crews more latitude on extra stops

Tipping

When U and L first started out rates were high enough and the company take was low enough that tipping really wasn't necessary. Today, rates have been slashed and both companies have increased their take to 25%, leaving drivers holding the mostly empty bag. L has always been more forward-thinking when it comes to tips, with a tip screen in the app. Drivers keep 100% of their tips on L and that is a highly attractive quality for drivers.

U riders are the worst tippers between the two services although they do tend to tip in higher amounts when they are inclined to part with some cash. I definitely ding U for cutting rates, raising their percentage and then only grudgingly relaxing their tip policy as quietly as possible. U is still telling customers that tipping is not necessary when drivers are, literally in some cases, starving. In my opinion U has not done enough to promote a culture of tipping since changing their rate structure. Imagine a restaurant paying its table service employees $15/hour and advertising that tipping is not necessary. Most people would think that was completely fair. Now imagine that same restaurant cuts table service wages to $2.90/hour and doesn't change the tip policy. That's exactly how drivers feel.

Most U customers still either believe that U drivers make a lot of money or that tips are included in the fare. My cynical side believes that, for most people, that's just a mental crutch they cling to because they don't want to bother carrying cash for tips or feel bad stiffing their driver.

I have not found any particular commonality when it comes to tipping, except that younger people tip less. Let's face it, when young people are struggling under a 10 year weight of student loan debt and stretching just to make their insane rent and house payments every month, I'll give them a pass. The rest of you, especially those of you in gated communities and luxury apartments, shame on you!

Part of your optimization strategy is then how to increase tips. In my experience driver rating and tips move in opposite directions. You can be popular and well-liked or make more money and get lower ratings. Striking a balance between the two is really hard.

Some drivers are getting aggressive about tips. Sending text messages ahead, calling attention to tip signs, demanding up front tips and other bad behaviors. That's another one of those unpredictable behaviors that's a consequence of lowering rates.

Tip Signs and Tip Jars

The two strategies drivers employ to deal with the tipping issue are tipping signs and tip jars.

Perhaps a bit obvious but it's your car being run into the ground and some people need a reminder.

As part of my research I tried several different car configurations that included tips signs and no tip signs. Just the plain car, with no bottled water or mints, netted a tip from roughly 20% of customers on both services. About one in five and that was fairly consistent over time. I used 20% as my baseline.

Then I tried bottled water and mints. That actually lowered the tip rate, which I believe is a statistical anomaly that would even out if I could afford to do this job long enough to get better data. It's safe to say that mints and water had no effect on the rate passengers tipped, so save the money.

Then I tried a tip sign like the one below:

That worked like a house on fire as far as tips go but my driver rating suffered. The sign positively nets more tips, my tip rate went from 20% to 30% in one day and has stayed fairly consistent since then, but my driver rating went down as well. The reminder seems to set up a kind of dissonance in the mind of the rider. They don't like being reminded that tips are not included in the fare. I see two possible reasons for that line of thinking: One is that many passengers still carry around company propaganda in their head that drivers make $75,000 to $90,000 a year. If you thought the driver was making a crapload of money and still working you for tips, you'd be rightly annoyed. The other is many passengers still think tips are included in the fare. Or, alternately, they don't have any cash and the sign makes them feel guilty.

Any of those reasons are enough for them to ding your driver rating. Sometimes the topic comes up when I've asked passengers about their passenger ratings. Many are surprised to find out they have a rating and even more surprised to discover that it can make a difference on getting a car. Most of the time low passenger ratings are associated with Pool riders, not tipping and gated communities.

Gated Communities

While we're on the subject...if you live in an area with few gated communities, then consider yourself lucky. Around here they're the bane of any driver's existence. Some are worse than others and I have not found a good solution. What I can say is people who live in gated communities tip far below the average. That may be because they get canceled a lot and they don't put together that getting canceled and not tipping for the gate wait are related.

Making money means avoiding guard gates as much as possible. Luckily, most are located far from urban centers. Once again we see that moving to an area with a higher population density and fewer gated communities is the key to consistently making more money.

Plan Your Drive Strategy

You'll discover that having your working outline setup before you head out will be key to increasing earnings. It's more than knowing where to hang out, it's also knowing how to avoid distractions and lowball fares that take you away from profitable work.

There's an old truism in the military that no battle plan survives contact with the enemy. I would tweak that a little to say that there's no plan for driving that survives your first ping. Your strategy is not going to be as clear once you get behind the wheel. You're trying to process a lot of information while also trying to drive safely, which has to take mental priority. Trust me when I say that in that environment your decision processes will not be as clear.

That's why the Watering Hole Strategy is so important. The less you have to think about your destination, the better. Have a list of productive areas and always be on the way toward one of them. Ignore as many Pool pings as you safely can and go offline if you need to escape being trapped by a series of Pool riders. Stay close to venues and areas where premium customers congregate and avoid the suburbs mid-morning which is when the Pool bottom feeders come out because they missed the bus. If you do get sucked into the suburbs, try to stay offline until you're sure the kids are in school so you don't have waste your time canceling an unaccompanied minor.

The other time to avoid is just before rush hour, when Pool riders try to beat the surge.

Being early to prime time isn't necessarily an advantage. Wait until the surge appears, then go online.

MUDDYING THE WATERS – GUARANTEED MINIMUMS AND BONUSES

We've already seen that, even when you know the rate card and population density, it can be hard to figure out just how much you're going to be able to make. Your actual income depends on a whole set of variables that include the number of hours you put in, your skill at avoiding certain types of customers, your service level, skill at navigating and ability to catch surge pricing. That's why even the most conservative income estimates often fall short.

We discussed previously how obscurity works in the company's favor, just like it works for casinos. If the normal unpredictability wasn't bad enough, both companies also offer guaranteed minimums and power driver bonuses.

Both companies use these incentives to try and lure drivers away from the other. It's hard to collect guaranteed minimums on U or bonuses on L if you're online with both apps trying to keep your car busy. The structure of the incentives make it nearly impossible to drive for both companies and collect those bonuses.

Not only that but the company pricing varies from state to state and sometimes region to region in the same state. The same trip taken in different states and at different times can have wildly different price tags for the rider and payouts for the driver. I believe the cloud of misinformation and disinformation is, in many ways, deliberate or, at best, coincidentally beneficial to the company.

Guaranteed Minimums

One of the most common incentives on U is called the guaranteed minimum. Guaranteed minimums work when you spend a certain amount of time in a certain area and are online picking up rides, the company will guarantee you a minimum hourly rate. While it sounds easy on paper, actually collecting on those guarantees can be really challenging. Many times drivers have to complain and challenge the company to collect. Imagine getting a payout line on a slot machine and then needing to fight with Casino Support to actually collect. Guaranteed minimums are another area of obscurity and we already know who benefits from that! Incentives are bait and you're the fish.

A guaranteed minimum seems easy enough. Pick up fares in a certain area at certain times, have an acceptance rate above 80% and stay online 50 minutes out of every hour to collect a minimum amount of money. That's where the simplicity ends and the fine print kicks in.

! Keep in mind incentives and the calculations change constantly !

Probably the biggest counter-intuitive aspect to the fine print of guaranteed minimums is that the hourly guarantee only applies to certain times, but U will use your hourly rate from other days of the week to adjust your incentive pay! Not just that, but L will count your tips toward your earnings to make that calculation. There are similar catches with all the other incentive criteria. If the minimum is one ride per hour, you have to average that over the entire week. That also isn't the end of the bad news. The guaranteed rate is before U takes its share. So, a $20 an hour incentive is actually $15.00. Sometimes that means U is taking a cut of money that you never actually earned.

There is a lot of fine print when it comes to collecting guaranteed minimums, so you have to read and understand the terms carefully. Sometimes the area is very specific and you can't always tell you're in the right place. Even if a ping comes while you're in the right area, that doesn't mean it originates in the right area. Guarantees are slippery and, the icing on the cake is they're not paid out until the following week. So, even if you earn a guaranteed minimum one week, you won't collect until the week after.

If that sounds like less of a good deal than it did a minute ago, then pat yourself on the back for catching on to guaranteed minimums.

I have never collected a guaranteed minimum, even when I tried, and many drivers are surprised when they do. Like with anything else associated with ride sharing, you'll find disinformation widely distributed in driver forums. There will inevitably be someone going on about how easy it was to make the minimum;

always in near-perfect English and always on a low activity account.

The perverse nature of guaranteed minimums flips your usual earning strategy on its head. Most of the time you're trying to maximize the number of rides per hour but, during times of guaranteed minimums, your strategy is to minimize the number of rides while collecting on the guarantees. You're trying to keep miles off your car and gas in your tank and still collect the money. If you earn more than the guaranteed minimum, you get no extra bonus.

When it comes to positioning, you want to start at a place where there are frequent requests for short trips to pick up your minimum number of rides. Once you have your minimum pickups, then you want to park in a low traffic area surrounded by other drivers and use them as a shield to make the balance of your 50 minutes as uneventful as possible.

Guaranteed minimums are, in my opinion, another example that the more you start tweaking a system, the more you have to twiddle with it to make it work. It's another layer of confusion and frustration for drivers trying to work in an already frustrating environment. Half the time collecting is as much luck as any particular skill on the driver's part. It's hard not to see the similarities in the incentive structure between the ride share industry and casinos.

U and L should just raise rates and drop all the shenanigans with guaranteed minimums and surge pricing. Customers hate surge pricing...hate it. Drivers hate trying to figure out the always elusive guaranteed minimums and chasing surge pricing is almost always a loser. The way I started viewing guaranteed minimums was using them as a guideline to where U and L think it will be busy.

Bonuses

Driver bonuses are structured so drivers picking up a lot of rides get a bonus. The structure is a little different between U and L but both companies offer them. I can't be more specific because driver bonuses are city and region specific. Usually the bonuses kick in somewhere around 75 rides and go up at different milestones.

Just like teasers at a casino, there are conditions attached to driver power bonuses. Sometimes they're limited to specific areas and a certain percentage of the rides have to originate in specific areas. I consider driver bonuses a sucker's game, like trying to beat the house at blackjack. You end up chasing around a lot and taking a lot of marginal rides for a couple hundred bucks. It's another example of how if U and L would just raise rates back to where they were and lower their cut, they could end all this nonsense.

The only bonus I collected was my $50 bonus for making 50 rides. Thinking of them like the giveaways at casinos is how I keep them in perspective.

RISK FACTORS

The essence of being in business for yourself is risk vs reward; that is the foundation of capitalism. Those who take the risks, those who build better mousetraps, reap the rewards. There are a lot of the very strong-willed independent types driving for U and L. In driver forums they'll tell you that if you work harder, work smarter than other people you'll make money. A few of those are company trolls but, surprisingly, many of them are sincere. Whether trolls or the seriously Libertarian, they are both completely wrong.

The problem with driving for U and L is it completely trashes the risk vs reward paradigm. Driving for any ride share company means you're accepting a great deal of risk for a fairly minimal reward. Some of the risks you'll face on a daily basis are not insignificant. U and L are happy to let you assume that risk and, in some cases, will even ding your driver rating for not accepting them.

Risk is one element but reward is another.

This is one business where working smarter and harder does not yield a better result. I proved that by actual experience. When ride sharing works best is when you find a way to game the system and make more money per ride while doing as little work as possible. On a fluke, one driver made nearly $20/hour on cancellations. Myself and every other driver would do that every day if it were possible. It's a cynical strategy but one that results in fewer miles on the car, less gas used and a decent hourly rate. The incentives in the current system encourage cheating, they encourage cherry picking and encourage collecting cancellation fees. Instead of having drivers invested in the success of the company, drivers do things like call ahead to find out where the customer is going and then drive around until the customer cancels if he or she doesn't like the destination.

Some of the risks outlined here are things you'll face on a daily basis and, in my experience, the company is largely deaf to driver concerns.

Unaccompanied Minors

This is a major problem and a huge source of potential liability. It's a liability issue because the company's insurance does not cover unaccompanied minors. Your personal auto insurance will also likely not cover them, either, leaving you personally responsible if they're injured. Every minor I refused to transport has told me they ride U and L all the time and I believe them because I've seen it with my own eyes. If it's questionable, I ask them if they're 18 on camera. There's nothing stopping them from lying but at least there would be evidence that I made a reasonable effort to establish the age of the rider.

Unaccompanied minors are not allowed by U's policy but I've never seen an account suspended because of it, either. L's policy is less clear, except in California where unaccompanied minors are not allowed in TNC vehicles. In discussions on driver forums the consensus seems to be that L is harder on the practice than U. The cherry on top is, of course, you'll get dinged for cancelling those rides unless you don't take the time to follow up with a complaint to driver support. Even then you won't get a cancellation fee for wasting your time, gas chasing a bad fare.

Bizarrely, drivers are forbidden from asking passengers for ID. You can ask their age but not demand proof. This is only one example of U putting drivers in a difficult position of potential liability. Either way you're going to get dinged somehow, the only question is how badly.

Account Name Mismatch

U and L are careful to make sure the person driving the car is who they claim to be, with U going so far as making spot check facial recognition on drivers before they can go online. But U and L are both totally okay with letting you as a driver ferry around a complete stranger using someone else's account.

The vast majority of the time such use is benign and being done as a convenience. I transported one young person supposedly named "Five" one night from a swanky gated community in North Palm Beach. I also transported four college age guys named "Diane" one Friday night, one of them explaining it was his mom's account. There have also been women using an account with a man's name and one guy named "Stephanie" who I cancelled and watched him chase the car down the street in the rear view mirror.

The big problem with account name mismatches is it's one of those touch points where ride sharing is no longer a community but a business...more specifically it's someone else's business. Taxi drivers deal with strangers in the car all the time but U and L are not taxi services and your car is not a cab. Ride share name mismatches means complete strangers are getting in your personal vehicle and U and L do not know who they are. When the person in your car is not the account holder the rider has no accountability for their behavior or any damage they do to your car.

Let's say you pick up some guy named "Angela" who mumbles something about using his girlfriend's account. If that person deliberately damages your car or makes a mess, Angela is the one who gets in trouble, not the person who actually did the damage. Angela is more likely to deny any involvement and claim the account use was fraudulent. Guess who gets stuck with the bill in those cases? I've personally had more trouble out of people coming along with the account holder, than actual account holders themselves who have contact information and a credit card on file with U and L.

Every single day or night that you drive, you will have an account/passenger mismatch. There are doctor's offices using U and L to transport patients to the office, people using U and L to shuttle their kids around, as we discussed above not all of them over 18, and boyfriends and girlfriends swapping accounts.

Is that guy using his girlfriend's account because it's convenient? Or is he using his cousin's account because he just got out of prison for a violent crime and can't get a credit card? With a rider name mismatch, you just never know.

The only way you can tell the difference between authorized use and fraudulent use is calling the account holder before letting the passenger in your car. That's an extra step, extra time and sometimes I'm just not in the mood to make that effort and cancel the rider. If it's a group of teenagers, I'm not even getting close enough to ask.

The problem is it's easy to get in the habit of just taking them, until the time comes that you're explaining to the cops that you just got robbed by some guy named Bridgette. When the rider is not the account holder, it's virtually impossible to trace them. Cab drivers face that risk all the time, as do bus drivers and train conductors. The difference is cab drivers know what they're signing up for, are insured to cover those contingencies and know how to manage that aspect of the business. Buses and trains have at least some security in the form of transit police.

To me the account holder mismatch is a bigger risk because it's so routine and U will ding your cancellation rate for not taking those rides. In that way the company, by their behavior, is putting less than subtle pressure on drivers to accept risky passengers.

False Accusations

Every week in a driver forum is someone with a story of woe that involves being falsely accused of inappropriate behavior by a passenger. Those accusations range from criticisms of driving to claims the driver said something to make them uncomfortable to unwanted touching. U & L suspend drivers first and investigate second. I get why they have to do that but that's lost work days while expenses roll on and there's no compensation for the driver, even if they're cleared.

Just this week I read about a driver who had a cab reverse into him at a stoplight and then file an injury claim. Around here that's a classic insurance scam, which is why we have dash cams in all our cars. Ride sharing without a dash cam, including an internal camera, is absolutely crazy. That footage can clear you of a false accusation. In rare cases that might include a police investigation if the charge is serious enough.

Without that proof it's your word against the passenger. U and L are notorious for siding with the passenger in a he-said-she-said situation. They have enough drivers they don't need to take a chance that report might be true.

What's the motivation of the false accuser? Sometimes they're just trying to scam free rides from U & L. That's all the motivation some people need.

Risk of Assault

Most U and L drivers don't worry about being assaulted but it nearly happened to me once, just after midnight on New Year's. Every week I can find a story in the local news about some altercation involving a U or L driver. Last week it was a U driver getting punched by a pissed off rider because the driver wouldn't let him bring more people than the car can legally hold. The week before an U driver and passenger were shot at during a ride. A few weeks before that a U driver shot and killed someone trying to carjack him. If you hear one story a week in an area the size of South Florida, then there are thousands of less serious confrontations that never get reported.

Drive long enough and it will happen to you. There will be some situation you feel threatened or intimidated. Nine out of ten times the problem is going to be someone who's been drinking. It's conflicting because people who use ride sharing instead of getting behind the wheel of a car after boozing it up are doing the right thing not driving drunk. All the same, if you're going to encounter a belligerent customer the chances are they're going to be drunk and more likely to be someone riding along with the account holder. The flip side to that coin is some of my best rides have been local drunks. Like with many things ride sharing it's a few bad actors ruining it for everyone and, as we discussed in the section on Ratings, you can't get rid of those few bad customers.

I'm comfortable with conflict and I'm large enough that no one is going to intimidate me physically. If you're not comfortable with conflict or easily pushed around, there will come that moment when a ride completely goes off the rails when a drunk bully gets in the car. Managing situations like that is one thing I can't cover in this book. If you can't deal with it, don't drive. Just know it is going to happen. You will face that situation.

Liability

There are a lot of stories on the internet about U and L drivers being found liable in accidents. Here's a good discussion about potential liability issues.

The good news, in small measure, is that the liability issues are better developed now than they were in the early days of ride sharing. More insurance companies in more states are offering ride share insurance or endorsements for your personal policy. Having ride share insurance is better than having nothing beyond a personal auto policy.

How Much Can You Afford To Lose?

It's really the liability issues that first got me rethinking whether it's a good idea to drive for U or L if you have something to lose, like a house, investments or savings. It might be wiser to form an LLC or corporate structure to protect your personal assets. But doing that just to drive for U or L is crazy, you'll never recoup those costs on ride sharing alone. Unless you're also operating as a limo service or some type of livery, it's unlikely you'll make enough money to cover your filing and reporting costs. There may be other ways to mitigate your personal liability, so it would be wise to talk to your lawyer and accountant if you have sizeable assets. Surprisingly, there are some bored wealthy people driving for U and L.

Personally, I believe the risks driving for U or L are mismatched for the reward. If drivers were allowed to set their own prices, as they would if they were really contractors, then you could set profitable rates, specific to the area you drive, and just not drive if you couldn't get them. As it is, with rates where they are today, your smartest bet is to do something else with your spare time.

Drugs and Alcohol

Motherboard did an interesting story on how U and L are changing the drug dealing landscape. A dealer making rounds with U and L is not risking having his or her car impounded, the risk as a driver is having your car impounded. Sure, we'd all like to think law enforcement would recognize the driver had nothing to do with it but I can point to plenty of instances where innocent people were swept up in routine enforcement actions. What makes you  think someone with drugs in your car isn't going to stash them between the seats, then act surprised and claim it was someone else in the car? Or agree to testify that it was you doing the drug dealing. If you're counting on the machine of criminal justice to get things right, you've already lost.

Some cities, like Gainesville, Florida, have clarified the rules about alcohol in a ride share car. But that doesn't apply statewide. The rule here in Florida is if an open container of alcohol is within the driver's reach, it's a $500 fine, points off your license and court costs. Like with the passenger drug issue, 99% of law enforcement would give the driver a break, it's that last 1% you're gambling your future on. Getting cited for an open container means you'd lose your ride share insurance and, the ultimate irony, U and L would both likely deactivate you. You'd also be paying higher insurance rates, basically forever.

Okay, most of these risks are low probability events and I'll certainly acknowledge that fact. I had hundreds of people in and out of my car with only a handful of issues. The problem is that it only takes one to seriously impact your life. Again, you're assuming that very real risk in a dead end job with limited returns. Put that time and effort into building a job that can grow into a living wage and has a future.

Think about it. If U and L were really such a great deal would they need to run TV commercials to get drivers?

ANNOYING PASSENGER TRICKS

Note: Most of these we've covered in previous sections but I wanted to put them all in one place and expand on some of them. You'll find out how important this chapter is if you start driving.

The most frustrating aspect of the ride share experience is managing problem passengers. These are people who act like you're driving a cab or company vehicle instead of hitching a ride in someone's personal car. I didn't have a separate column for tracking problem passengers but I'd say roughly 10%-20% fall into that category.

The other 80%-90% are people I would hang around with outside of U or L. I've met professionals from all walks of life, all races and ethnic backgrounds. The vast majority are people that I found both entertaining and engaging.

U and L Complicate The Problem

We have previously covered the ratings issue. By allowing bad ratings to stand, U is putting pressure on drivers to allow passengers to do things that are unprofitable, dangerous and, sometimes, illegal. The company, of course, would deny that in public statements but their behavior behind the scenes speaks louder than the PR department. I was still driving after the big announcement about the company taking a harder look at passenger behavior, but nothing much has really changed. Now the person who made that announcement has left the company.

Even when you cancel a passenger for cause, U and L still count it against your cancellation rate. Just in my experience, U has raised my cancellation rate for the following things:

- Cancelling because a customer was in a gated community and wouldn't answer their phone and I couldn't get past the guard shack
- Canceling an unaccompanied minor
- Canceling a Pool customer with an exceptionally low user rating
- Cancelling because a customer wanted to bring an open alcohol container into my car
- Canceling because the customer entered the wrong address and I couldn't find them
- Canceling a customer who clearly was not the account holder

So, just about any time you take a stand for what's right, you'll be penalized for it. But do keep in mind the fundamental rule: The penalty from a high cancellation rate is better than the penalty for low driver ratings or a judgment.

Alcohol

The biggest challenge I face on a regular basis is passengers trying to bring alcohol into the car or open containers. Alcohol in cars is also a violation of U's Terms and Conditions (T&C) but drivers do not enforce the T&C uniformly. Some, who may be struggling with a low driver rating, are afraid to make an issue out of it with passengers. In that sense, U's driver rating system is reinforcing potentially illegal and dangerous behavior. At a minimum it's rude and thoughtless and passengers report that U drivers are roughly 50/50 about allowing alcohol.

Seriously, you can't stop drinking for 12 minutes to get from your apartment to the restaurant? I hate those passengers and positively will drive away and leave them. If you want to drink that badly hire a limo or the party bus. They're licensed and insured for that activity, your U and L drivers are not.

Passengers In a Rush

Passengers in a hurry are more likely to call ahead and tell you they're in a hurry. They're behind and trying to make it your problem. I absolutely will not speed or break traffic laws for a customer, regardless of the money or motivation. Instead I remind them that my job is to get them there safely. Surprisingly, that usually works. There are numerous stories in the press about the company monitoring driver behavior behind the wheel, including speeding and hard braking. That monitoring is positively going on when passengers are in the car and may be going on even when drivers are off the clock.

The in a hurry crowd are more likely to give you a low driver rating, so you have to make a judgment call on whether you can get them there on time. If you know you can't get there in time, canceling is better than letting them in your car when their urgency will become your problem to manage.

Too Many People For The Car

This is one you sometimes get paid a cancellation fee. It's illegal and it violates U's T&C but people still try to avoid the higher prices of an XL or SUV by squeezing a +1 in an X car. It boggles the mind that some drivers accommodate this behavior, especially considering the driver would get the ticket. Since I can screen them out before they get in the car, it doesn't bother me. Cancellation fees are easy money. Drive away and cancel for too many people.

Underage Persons Using a Parent's Account

This is a big one and fraught with potential liability. Busy parents are trying to use U and L like a school bus. I am absolutely amazed how many drivers don't even bother to ask younger looking passengers if they're 18. Under U's Terms and Conditions, an unaccompanied minor using an older adult's account is a clear no-no and is fraudulent use of an account. All the same, even when you report unaccompanied minors, U or L rarely deactivate their rider account.

Group accounts and letting someone else use their account is also not allowed but you will meet a account holder/rider mismatch every single time you go out. This is a major problem and one time I wish U would structure the service to fit the reality of how the system is being used. I'd be happy to drop your kids at school if I knew insurance covered the trip and I had the parent's explicit permission to transport an unaccompanied minor.

Amazingly, many drivers transport passengers without bothering to ask if they're the account holder. If those passengers are minors, you're taking a huge liability risk. Unfortunately, many ride share drivers come from other countries where liability is less strict. By not asking you may be incurring liability and, in some extreme circumstances, risk of arrest.

This is why I have video operating inside the car. If a passenger lies on camera that they're 18 or lies that they're the account holder, that at least gives me a small measure of protection.

Small Children, No Car Seat

I've had parents lie to me about their kid's age. "Oh, she's six, she's just small." Right. More like she's four and you don't have a car seat. One driver has a clipboard with the child seat and open container regulations taped to the bottom. That's a great idea. Don't argue with me, tell it to the clipboard.

Nice Account Holder, Belligerent Fellow Passenger

This is the most vexing kind of problem you'll encounter. A problem account holder can be removed from the system if their behavior is bad enough but what happens when the account holder is nice and one of the people with them is the jerk? You can certainly report them but, if you do, then the nice person gets the ban hammer, the cleaning fee and sued for damages.

This happened to me just after midnight on New Year's Day. A mean drunk bullied a nice passenger for a ride...without asking me. He then tries to bring three other girls with him, for a total of five people. Five people in an X violates both the law and U's T&C. I told him four was the limit and that's where the trouble began. He slammed the car door, scratching it in the process and got pissy with me.

Fortunately, I can take care of myself and he walked away but if I reported that incident, then the nice guy would have his account suspended. I realized that your options narrow very quickly and sometimes there are no good answers. The obvious answer is call 911, right? Okay, that's 4 or 5 minutes waiting for the cops. Then a long time trying to explain to the cops what happened while they sort through four or five different stories, only one of which is yours. In my experience the police have never improved a situation. Just like in politics if you're explaining, you're losing.

A good dash cam, one that also has an interior camera, is necessary to support your version of events. In hindsight the situation won't be nearly as clear as they seem at the time.

Canceling In The Middle Of a Ride

This one just mystifies me but it happens. You'll transport someone to their original destination and you get there only to find you're online waiting for rides instead of the drop off screen. I had that happen at least once, probably more than once. After a while I got better at hearing the cancelation audio alert. If someone does that to you, take them to nearest safe drop off location. Don't dump them on the side of the highway, take the next exit and kick them out at a gas station or other safe spot. Do NOT give them a chance to claim it was an accident and enter the correct address. Never give a problem customer a second bite at the apple. People who do that are not stealing from the company, they're stealing from drivers. That's just pathetic.

Illegal Activities

There are people using U and L to facilitate drug deals and other illegal activities. That's probably true of any transportation system and ride sharing is no different. The difference is those other transportation services usually have some type of legal protection while you do not. You as the driver can get in trouble or have your car impounded. If I get the slightest whiff of anything sketchy, end the ride as soon as possible. Don't be afraid to cancel and drive away. You have to protect yourself first and that's more important than your driver rating or a crappy, low-paying job.

If you do have a problem with a passenger, for whatever reason, the smart strategy is file a complaint with Driver Support right away.

! When it comes to a bad passenger or ride, it's better to be the first to complain. U tends to side with whoever complains first !

A few other passenger behaviors are less of a problem.

Vaping

Most people are smart enough to stuff out their cigarette before getting in a car but some people think nothing of releasing a cloud of vapor in your car. I don't react as strongly to someone vaping as I would them trying to light up a cigarette, but it gives my sinuses fits and leaves an oil film on the window interiors that's hard to get off.

Taking Over The Entertainment System

This happens a surprising number of times. A passenger will want access to the car entertainment system's auxiliary input. I finally ordered an aux connector cable. I'm okay with this but I insist on pulling over to connect the device so I'm not distracted while trying to drive. I've been exposed to music that I wouldn't have heard in any other context. Most of it doesn't fit my tastes but it's good to expose your senses to music and art outside your personal comfort zone.

Puking

I usually knock off before the really drunk people start heading home so I've been lucky about not having people throw up in the car. If you drive long enough, it will happen. A passenger might be sick and trying to get to the doctor and you're their only way of getting there. You should be prepared for it, even if you don't drive during closing time at the bars. See the chapter on Accessories for cleaning supplies and vomit bags.

I was a volunteer EMS/firefighter for five years so I try to be a little understanding if someone can't make it. I've dealt with some nasty biologicals in my day, so a little vomit barely registers. The cleaners I have listed are ones that remove stains and mask odors and I discovered one of them by accident.

Protect Yourself

Your best insurance is having a video camera in the car. I have a dash cam with a rear camera. Instead of mounting the rear camera in the back window, I mounted it on the visor. There I can see what's happening inside the car and the traffic situation outside. No matter what happens, there will be a record. Seeing the camera is all it takes for most people to realize that being stupid and trying to talk their way out of it later will be a loser.

The two issues that really motivated me to get out of ride sharing were insurance and that 10% of problem passengers. Honestly, the problem passengers would have been enough all by themselves. The thoughtlessness and sheer gall of some people was astounding.

THE FATAL FLAW

In the Intro I promised to tell you why I think the ride sharing industry, as it exists today, is not going to survive. I wanted to put this bit near the end so people who aren't interested in my opinion of the industry can skip it.

Nowhere To Go But Down

Yes, I understand that the number of ride share rides are continuing to grow but that doesn't change my opinion that the industry as whole has peaked and what lies ahead are declining fortunes.

The reason I believe the ride share industry will ultimately fail is rooted in the history of the service itself. In the beginning ride sharing was an outgrowth of the sharing economy. People who had things, like a lawn mower, could rent that to their neighbors for a small fee. That way two or three families could share a lawn mower and one person got extra money to maintain the resource and keep it in good working order. The middleman was a matchmaker organization that kept a small percentage of the payment to cover their expenses.

The sharing economy was not initially about making money, though quite a few of the early adopters of the sharing economy did make money and a few made a lot of money. Over time the sharing economy gradually morphed into more of a rental economy and became more structured.

One of the services that popped up in the sharing economy was ride sharing. People with cars opened up those empty seats to people who needed a ride. The early days were more like high tech carpooling. When U came along, all that changed. Instead of carpooling, ride sharing became on-demand transportation. As ride sharing grew into an enterprise, the community aspect of it was pushed to the side. Ride sharing went corporate and business users flooded into the system because it was more convenient than a cab.

Corporate interests gradually took over on the driver side as well and U, the dominant company in the space, slashed rates to try and attract more riders and did so without any input from the community of drivers. At nearly the same time the company launched out on an ambitious and expensive program to develop self-driving cars to replace drivers. Not only was ride sharing not a community anymore but the dominant corporate interest made it known, by deed if not word, that drivers were an inconvenient expense. To keep competition from taking hold, U slashed rates again a year later, which again slashed driver pay and L cut its rates to stay competitive. In an attempt to train riders for the new future of automated transportation, both U and L implemented services where users shared a car with other passengers going the same direction. The company greatly discounted the shared service but the few pennies riders saved were largely coming out of the pockets of drivers.

The new rate structure, coupled with discount services, destroyed what was left of the community aspect of ride sharing. Due to the new incentive structure, drivers and passengers are frequently at odds with one another on individual transactions. Passengers today are trying to save a couple bucks at the expense of drivers already operating very near a net loss. Many times I could feel the tension in the car as riders tried to insulate themselves from any suggestion that they were using a service that drivers hated. For Line and Pool riders, ignorance is indeed bliss.

Drivers fought back against the discount services and discount passengers by just not taking Pool and Line riders. Soon the situation escalated to near war with their own drivers, the people they're working hard to get rid of, and the drivers fought back.

Instead of driving directly to the Pool passenger, drivers take the scenic route, adding minutes to the pickup time until the customer gets annoyed and cancels. Sometimes the driver will park somewhere the car is difficult to see and cancel if the passenger can't find them. The experienced drivers started making Pool rides as inconvenient and unreliable as possible without being bumped off the system. U was discovering that you can't win a war against your own partners and yet the company clings to the hated service because the company makes more money.

The reduced rates introduced other unpredictable behaviors to the system. Drivers started calling ahead to see where passengers were going. If it was a short ride, they would stall until the rider gave up and canceled or just cancel them outright. If it was too long of a trip to an area where the driver had to come back empty, the rider would also get cancelled, sometimes two or three times in a row. The practice is called "cherry picking" and it's now ubiquitous in the ride share industry. U and L have made token attempts to stop the practice but, since a majority of the really good drivers have adopted the practice, U and L would be cutting their most profitable drivers. There's also the problem both companies will have if they're seen trying too hard to control driver behavior, which could prompt the government to rule drivers are employees entitled to minimum wage and benefits. U and L would be in a tight financial spot overnight if that happened.

Surge pricing is another layer that puts the company, drivers and passengers at odds with one another. Instead of having fixed days and times when rates are higher, the company calculates surge pricing basically on the fly. Passengers resort to constantly refreshing the app or canceling if they get a surge rate. Drivers start ignoring non-surge pings in an effort to squeeze a couple dollars more out of each ride. Prime time price surges turn into a giant game of Dump The Chump, with riders and drivers canceling rides for different reasons. The current implementation of surge pricing is another crystal clear example of misaligned incentives.

Every time a passenger cancels a surge fare, every time a driver stalls a Pool rider, every time drivers cancel short rides or extended return trips, the system becomes a little less reliable. When reliability slips, so does customer confidence. It may be anecdotal but I hear the reliability concern a lot from my passengers. A few have gone back to cabs for short rides from the airport after being canceled three or four times in a row on short rides to a nearby hotel.

The new dynamic, that largely developed between 2014 and 2015, is mostly dysfunctional, with incentives for passengers, drivers and the company completely out of alignment. That dysfunctional incentive alignment is why I see the ride share industry ultimately failing. Robotic cars are not going to fix passenger behavior, I believe instead they will compound the problem.

It's Not a Transportation System

So far we've talked about the misaligned incentive structure and how cutting rates resulted in random and unexpected behaviors by drivers but the real diamond core that can't be changed is the fact that ride sharing is trying to stretch to become a transportation system and it was never intended to fill that role.

Ride sharing is not a transportation system to me; to me it's my car. U and L are trying to replace public transportation with an on-demand system that relies upon my car. The problem that U and L will never overcome is that I'm not going to allow just anyone in my car. Once a group of kids with open drinks and bags of snacks got a rude surprise when I told them they weren't bringing their food and open drinks in my car. I drove off and left them standing in front of the store. The same with the couple I saw arguing out in front of a restaurant and just kept going. Or the under 21 enterprising young man in a swanky gated community who ended up trying to chase me down the street on foot carrying two six packs of bottle beer. Not a chance in hell was I taking that rider. I've also turned down riders using someone else's account, using what were obviously fake accounts, unaccompanied minors and people who just crawled out from under a dirty job and thought they were going to put their dirty work pants on my tan seats. Guess again.

Those stories are relatively minor in comparison to what other drivers face on a daily basis. There are the pukers, the ones who smell, bad breath, food odors, the guy using his girlfriend's account because he just got out of prison and a whole host of people that no sane and reasonable person would want in their car. The bus may have to take anyone with enough money to make the fare but ride share drivers don't get paid enough to take chances and they will cancel the rider if they don't like what they see.

All of that inherent conflict will prevent ride sharing from becoming an on-demand mass transportation system. U and L will never build a mass transportation infrastructure with hundreds of thousands of contractors driving privately owned vehicles. The company also knows that's true and I believe that knowledge is the key motivation behind the push toward autonomous vehicles. That will solve the driver problem but will also bring along a whole new set of problems for the company. Like whether users will accept self-driving cars. If my passengers are any indication, there's going to be a learning curve. Many are skeptical of the reliability of self-driving cars and suspicious of them.

Autonomous cars will not care if someone is using a friend or family member's account, they won't care if a passenger smells or has dirt and grease on his or her clothing. You can bet that the next passenger following them into that autonomous car will care and will go ballistic when that grease, blood and dirt gets on their clothing. And, believe me, those are not the worst things that people are going to leave behind on autonomous car seats.

The other problem for the company will be owning the car. That means owning fuel, insurance and maintenance costs. U and L discovering the time and effort it takes just to clean up after messy passengers is going to be a revelation all by itself. People can be disgusting. People will do disgusting things in their autonomous vehicles and treat them with contempt. Those seats will be sticky for the worst imaginable reasons.

Looking at it from that standpoint, drivers suddenly don't look as bad. I know as well as anyone that driverless cars will not only be the reality in a few short years, they'll be the preferred way to travel. Personally, I can't wait. Instead of letting that market develop naturally and be shaped by market forces, U and L are trying the shape the future of the transportation industry, an effort that is almost certain to end in failure. People want their own car and that's not going to change just because the car steers itself.

Every passenger who has ridden with me because they had car problems or were in an accident, couldn't wait to get their car back. Even if U and L cost much less than owning a car, most people still want their own personal transportation space. That's the problem that U and L's driverless cars cannot fix.

I want a self-driving car but I don't necessarily want to share it with anyone, for the same reason I don't like riding the bus. I don't want to sit next to icky people or their smells and I'm willing to pay to avoid doing so. I realize that sounds snobbish and I know the vast, vast majority of people are entirely decent. The problem is not people in general, it's a mere handful of bad passengers. Of the hundreds of people in and out of my car less than a dozen were the problem riders. Yet their influence is outsized compared to their numbers. Those same smelly, dirty, drunk, sick and mentally unbalanced people who tried to get in my car, will be getting in next to you in U's self-driving cars. A relative few will spoil it for the many. Spend some time in a New York subway if you want to know what the inside of a driverless cab is going to look like.

Let's take the human component out of it so it doesn't seem so bigoted or snobbish and replace the people with things. I don't want to sit next to puke, urine, saliva, sweat, blood, semen, body odor or anything else that routinely comes out of a human body. I don't want to sit next to lice, fleas or bedbugs. If you're honest, you'll admit that you don't want to sit next to those things, either. There's nothing snobby about appreciating the joys of modern hygiene, a happiness that is not shared equally by all our fellow travelers.

The company would argue that cameras in the cars will keep most people from getting out of hand (or maybe it's better to say in hand) but I would argue whether that's true. I have a friend in California who works for one of the coastal cities south of Los Angeles. They have cameras set up in public spaces and he's one of the people who monitors them. He has quite a collection of video clips that show people sleeping and masturbating in elevators, having sex in public places and throwing up almost everywhere. A few are doing do so in full knowledge they're being recorded, even putting on a show for the cameras in some cases. This same behavior, the less glamorous side of human nature that proves we're really just one step removed from our animal ancestors, goes on, to a greater or lesser extent, everywhere.

It's not a lot of people, a mere handful (there I go with that pun again) but that handful can positively spoil any public space or transportation system. Cameras are not going to stop people from drinking, screwing and doing other obnoxious things in self-driving cars.

Passenger Risk

Riding in U cars while we're awaiting our driverless future is also getting to be more risky, even if you make it through the call-ahead screening and don't get cancelled. If you're in a large urban center there's a better chance these days that your driver has been behind the wheel 10 or 12 hours, or longer, or that he's been sharing a cheap hotel room with other U drivers to take naps and showers while chasing his or her incentive numbers. The rate cuts are pushing drivers to do crazy things to make enough money to survive and stretch for ever more difficult driver bonuses.

In many places your driver may be new to this country and not have a good command of English. He or she is driving ride share because they don't have any other employment options. Around here there's less of that. We're far enough from urban centers that here many drivers are retirees looking to make some extra cash and get out of the house. Those are, in many ways, the perfect U and L drivers but the pace of traffic is too fast in more urban areas and there are fewer retirees willing to risk Miami traffic chasing bingo money.

Keep in mind that U still has to survive another three to five years with human drivers and, right now, I don't see how the company will ever be able to borrow enough money to get to that future. Trying to turn ride sharing into an enterprise just isn't working from where I stand. U should drop the autonomous car research, raise rates and go back to being a middleman. U and L both need to stop trying to compete with public transportation and letting passengers game the platform.

Yet I know for a certainty that U and L will never fix those problems because they already are driving hard toward what they see as the future. In the quest for tomorrow they're overlooking the necessity to survive today and the company is compounding their problems by taking on massive amounts of debt.

I've read many people comparing U to Amazon. Okay, granted that operating a company at a loss while still growing is how companies eventually reach critical mass and turn profitable enough to pay back all that VC money. The difference is Amazon recorded a few quarterly losses and one bad year while it was growing, it did not record year after year of major losses. The one bad year it did have, Amazon responded by cutting its workforce by 15% and slashing expenses. U has been bleeding cash since day one and, as the years go by, the debt and losses continue to mount. Amazon was never subsidizing 60% of the cost of the product it was selling.

Cultural Issues

We've all seen the stories in the news about the cultural problems at U, which I would argue are common to Silicon Valley as a whole. I agree that these issues are a distraction but it's a distraction that comes at a time when the company must perform perfectly in order to survive long enough to make it to their self-driving future. The #DeleteU movement really stung the company, with more than 200,000 people deleting the passenger app in just one weekend.

Beyond being a hostile working environment for women, rumors suggest there is considerable internal conflict between departments. I've seen that conflict before in other large, fast-growing companies and that lack of coordinated direction ends up robbing the companies of both momentum and operating capital. The internal conflict of the company is mirrored all the way down to the street level. The incentives for the company, the drivers and passengers put every element of the transaction at odds with one another.

Personally, I'd like to have a service like U available for the odd times I need it. Even if the rates were higher. The convenience and atmosphere still make it preferable to a cab. When my wife and I call a car, we're ready to go, have a foot on the curb and we have tipped every single one of our U drivers. But we'll stop using the service when it becomes unreliable. We'll stop using it when drivers call ahead to see if the trip is worth it and then get charged a cancellation fee when they finally stall us into submission. We'll stop when our driver doesn't speak English and the car smells like curry. We'll stop when the driver is wired to ceiling slamming energy drinks because he or she has been behind the wheel for 14 hours. Mainly we'll stop using the service when a better alternative comes along, even if it costs more.

For cab and car companies, I would encourage them not to quit in the face of U and L but to learn from them. There would be many ways to compete with both major ride share companies, though you'll have to do it for less than $3.00 a mile. You don't have to beat U and L on price, just offer a better experience.

Those are the reasons I don't see the ride share industry surviving. While visionary leaders at U still get the credit for creating a disruptive transportation technology, they'll also own the blame when it collapses. What got me out of ride sharing were unsustainable insurance costs and undesirable passengers. Overall, it's just not a good deal for drivers anymore and that will continue to weigh the industry going forward.

QUESTIONS & ANSWERS

These are questions friends and neighbors asked me about driving for U and L. I thought I'd share the answers as kind of a wrap up. If you're a journalist and need a quote, you can use any of these in the context of your article. Just don't paraphrase so it changes the meaning and I'll back up a fact check. There's contract information in the About The Author section.

Would I Do It Again?

I'm not sure. I'm definitely not doing it if insurance costs $1,800 every six months. If I could get ride share coverage for a premium over my regular insurance, then I might consider going back occasionally during high demand events. What I positively won't do is just go out and take just any rides. I might work the cruise ship port, the airport and special events for a little extra cash but ferrying drunks, underage partiers and college kids on Friday and Saturday nights is not happening.

It also depends on whether U and L have

taken any steps to address the routine risks, which I doubt they're going to do. I'd also weigh whether U has done anything to start encouraging tipping. That still ranks as the biggest sticking point with drivers.

I should note that none of my family want me to go back to driving.

What Was The Best Thing To Come Out Of Your Experience Driving?

The car. The more I drive my Prius, the more I'm convinced it's one of the greatest pieces of automotive engineering ever fielded. You'd have to pry my 4 wheel drive pickup out of my cold, dead hands but I totally get why Prius owners are so devoted.

What Would I Do Different Next Time?

Not much. I did a ton of research before going out the first time and pretty much nailed it out of the gate. The only difference is I might get a top of the line dash cam with the infrared camera to keep a better eye on passengers in the dark.

What Was Your Strangest Customer?

That would be Christmas Eve strip club couple. I picked up this pair outside a restaurant in North Palm on Christmas Eve with the destination being a local strip club. She's drunker than he is and bawdy as all get out, but she's funny and it was mostly entertaining. When we get there we discovered the strip club was closed. After much debate we tried two more clubs, both of them also closed. Not to be deterred from getting their lap dance on they proceeded to call around to the other clubs until they actually found one open until 5 am on Christmas day. I now know that if you want a lap dance on Christmas Eve, the Spearmint Rhino is your only option around here.

I never realized there were so many strip clubs in this county until I started driving.

What Was Your Worst Customer?

There's a lot of competition for that coveted spot. That award probably goes to a guy named Rafa and his date that I picked up at a Palm Beach hotel. They were late getting to a party boat at the boat docks downtown. He kept reminding me they were in a hurry, which does nothing but annoy me. While he's doing that his ditzy girlfriend, who is wearing perfume strong enough to kill insects, is on the phone going on endlessly about how fantastic the parties are in Miami. After long minutes of listening to her prattle on he starts vaping in my car without asking and trying to hide it. Since we're almost there I decided not to make an issue of it. I get what's called a "slam" which is another reservation for the car after I drop them off, so the car is already booked when we get to the address they entered but there's no dock. Panic sets in because they're both high, late and at the wrong address. They keep describing the boat to me as if that will make it magically appear. They finally call the company running the boat and figure out it's another mile downtown. We make our way down there and, by some miracle of driving, I manage to still get them there on time. Instead of the least bit of gratitude, the pair dash out of the car without tipping. The icing on the cake was the people waiting for the car canceled because it was taking too long. In hindsight I should have kicked the ungrateful bastards out at their destination address and let them walk the rest of the way.

Those two were representative of so many bad passenger qualities that they get the award for the worst. I was lucky. Most drivers could do a lot worse when it comes to bad passenger stories.

Is It Fun?

Some days and some customers, yeah, there were fun rides. Most of the time it wasn't that much fun. It was just a job and the best I could hope for most days was that something bad wouldn't happen. Overall there is too much fighting. Fighting with driver support, being constantly on guard against stupid passenger tricks, canceling sketchy looking customers, unaccompanied minors and account name mismatches. Even when everything else goes right, you still have to deal with the passenger's sense of entitlement. You never really know what people are like until you work a low level service job.

What Was The Most Frustrating Aspect Of Driving?

There were two aspects that I found equally frustrating. The first was driver ratings. Getting a low rating happens to everyone but it still hurts your feelings, unless you're a complete psycho (and some of the drivers are). Many other frustrations are related to that core issue. Like U deactivating a driver for merest suggestion of wrongdoing but ignoring the Fraudulent Use cancellation instead of suspending the rider account. Rider ratings should count for more. Low rated riders should get kicked off the platform just like low-rated drivers. And don't let them simply create another account and get back on the system. Kick them off and make it stick.

The other frustrating aspect was getting to the passenger, sometimes after a 10 or 12 minute drive with a stop at the security shack of a gated community, only to find the passenger was someone you either can't or didn't want to take. A couple of those and you'll hang it up for the night.

What's The Scariest Thing That Happened To You?

The underage drinking party on New Year's Eve at a poorly lit gated community in Jupiter. That's as close as I ever came to needing any of the defensive weapons I carried. Drive long enough and someone will try to intimidate or bully you. One Orlando driver I know from the driver forums was stabbed in the arm during an altercation with a passenger with a knife. Another driver in West Palm got punched in the face for refusing to take more passengers than his car could hold. U and L both have policies against drivers carrying guns but, if you live in a state with concealed carry, your safety comes before a low-paying, high-risk sideline job. It's easy to say "no guns" when you work in a secure office in downtown San Francisco. When you're by yourself on a poorly lit street off NW 15th Ave in Fort Lauderdale on a Saturday night, it's an entirely different calculation.

Would You Let Your Wife Or Family Member Drive For a Ride share Service?

Not a chance.

What Do The Major Ride Services Have Right?

While sporadic problems with the app are normal, for both drivers and passengers, overall both U and L operate very robust systems that can keep functioning even during times of heavy demand. Sometimes the fare and pay calculations will be backed up but the app keeps working, even during the busiest times. There are a lot of upstart competitors out there but none of them match U and L's reliability and uptime. Anyone who has ever built an enterprise scale application can appreciate how hard that is to do.

What Advice Do You Have For Riders?

Surprisingly, I get asked that a lot. First, keep in mind that the driver is getting pennies to wait on you, so be outside by the time the car gets there. Identify yourself and let them know that this is everyone before you reach for the door handle. Once inside the car remain aware you're in some other person's car, not a cab or commercial vehicle. Act like you would in a friend's car. Don't ask for an extra stop unless you're willing to tip in advance. Call another car when you're done with your errand. If you're in a busy location, it probably won't take that long. And always make sure you have cash for a tip. I took a guy 1.5 miles and he still tipped me $2.00. Those are golden customers and a couple in a row can make your night much more tolerable.

If You Were CEO Tomorrow, What Would You Change?

Step one would be changing the company's culture. U is fixated on competition both internally and externally. The basketball and football coaches with the winning records don't focus on the competition, they focus on excellence. The same is true in the business world where the most successful companies build a culture of excellence. I'd rather have the second best engineer in the world who's a team player and builds up his or her subordinates than the best engineer in the world who creates an uncomfortable environment for coworkers.

On the business front I'd stop trying to compete for the low end of the market and focus on higher tier customers. Let competitors have the bottom feeders and mass transit refugees. That would certainly mean more local competition but no one is going to build a competitive empire on city bus riders. There's a reason we have to subsidize public transportation.

Then I'd end the autonomous car research. Everyone and their dog is working on driverless cars; I haven't seen anything like it in technology since the Dot Com boom. Driverless cars are certainly going to happen, but I'd rather be second in that market than pioneer the customer resistance challenges. To me it would be better to lease the technology from a partner when it's more mature than try to carry the overhead of development.

After that I would raise fares, a lot, and cherry pick the best drivers and passengers. As part of the fare restructuring, I'd fix surge pricing to certain times of the day and specific events. I'd also drop the company take to 20 percent, fix it there and add a tip screen. I'd remake U back into a lean middleman supplying transportation technology. That could even mean leasing branded technology services to potential competitors. Think about who makes the real money in retail. It's not the brick and mortar store, it's the companies handling the banking transactions on the backend. VISA gets a cut of nearly everything you buy. That's where I'd rather be in the technology space, not dealing with John Q Public.

Finally, I'd make passenger ratings actually count and recognize that ride sharing is not for everyone. I'd make passengers periodically verify their identity, just like drivers. I might stop short of background checks for passengers but anyone who can't compose themselves or stop drinking for 12 minutes would find themselves back in a cab. And I'd either require the account holder to be present during the ride or insist they create a user account for authorized riders. I would reshape U and L into more of a club than a service and the master account holder would be 100 percent responsible for the behavior of their guests in the car.

Any Parting Thoughts?

The only thing keeping the major ride share businesses going is the convenience factor of being able to work anytime you have a few minutes. I would encourage other companies to be more creative about scheduling. Provide a flexible work environment that pays a steady $20 an hour and I'll have U and L drivers lined up around the block to apply. Those are people who passed a 50 state background check. Too few companies are leveraging technology to build a flexible working environment.

For people thinking of driving...if you're doing it strictly for some extra cash, it's an okay job most nights. If you're thinking of quitting a paying job to drive ride share, forget that right now. Don't quit any job to drive ride share. There's just too much risk and not enough reward to make it worthwhile. Before you put your car and driving record on the line for a small return, invest in a book called The $100 Startup by  Chris Guillebeau. See if a book like that can spark an idea where you can build a small sideline gig for yourself that pays better and provides more job satisfaction.

ABOUT THE AUTHOR

Chris Poindexter is a freelance writer and photographer living along Florida's Treasure Coast. His past jobs include nuclear research for the Department of Energy and building data systems for the U.S. Navy. His current writing customers include a variety of magazines and online periodicals.

His non-fiction books include My House Has Wheels which documents his four year adventure living full-time in an RV. Another non-fiction book coming out soon is 10,000 Miles In Town, about the quest to build the perfect city bike.

He also has a fiction series, set in the sultry, steamy world of South Florida. Many of the fictional characters in his books are based on composites of real people. A fan of John D.

 MacDonald, his writing style is influenced by the Travis McGee mystery series, though updated to account for more modern technology and the faster pace of modern life.

Send any text corrections, comments and any math mistakes to info(at)chrispoindexter(dot)com. I really do monitor that address and will do my best to respond.

www.ingramcontent.com/pod-product-compliance
Lightning Source LLC
Chambersburg PA
CBHW071429180526
45170CB00001B/274